The Discourse on the Fruits of Recluseship

The Sāmaññaphala Sutta and its Commentaries

Translated from the Pali
by
Bhikkhu Bodhi

BPE

BPS Pariyatti Editions

BPS Pariyatti Editions
An imprint of Pariyatti Publishing
www.pariyatti.org

Published by Buddhist Publication Society, Kandy, Sri Lanka, 1989, 2004, 2008.

Published with the consent of the original publisher.

First BPS Pariyatti Edition, 2022
ISBN: 978-1-68172-497-3 (Print)
ISBN: 978-1-68172-498-0 (PDF)
ISBN: 978-1-68172-499-7 (ePub)
ISBN: 978-1-68172-500-0 (Mobi)
LCCN: 2022946079

CONTENTS

Translator's Preface v

Texts Used viii

List of Abbreviations ix

Introduction 1

Part One: The Text of the Sāmaññaphala Sutta 19

Statements of the Ministers 19
The Statement of Jīvaka Komārabhacca 20
The Question on the Fruits of Recluseship 21
The Doctrine of Pūraṇa Kassapa 22
The Doctrine of Makkhali Gosāla 23
The Doctrine of Ajita Kesakambala 25
The Doctrine of Pakudha Kaccāyana 26
The Doctrine of Nigaṇṭha Nātaputta 27
The Doctrine of Sañjaya Belaṭṭhaputta 28
The First Visible Fruit of Recluseship 29
The Second Visible Fruit of Recluseship 31
The More Excellent Fruits of Recluseship 32
The Small Section on Moral Discipline 33
The Intermediate Section on Moral Discipline 35
The Large Section on Moral Discipline 39
Restraint of the Sense Faculties 42
Mindfulness and Clear Comprehension 43
Contentment 43
The Abandoning of the Hindrances 43
The First *Jhāna* 45
The Second *Jhāna* 46
The Third *Jhāna* 46
The Fourth *Jhāna* 47
Insight Knowledge 47
The Knowledge of the Mind-made Body 48
The Knowledge of the Modes of Supernormal Power 49
The Knowledge of the Divine Ear 50
The Knowledge Encompassing the Minds of Others 50

The Knowledge of Recollecting Past Lives 51
The Knowledge of the Divine Eye 52
The Knowledge of the Destruction of the Cankers 54
King Ajātasattu Declares Himself a Lay Follower 55

Part Two: The Commentarial Exegesis of the Sāmaññaphala Sutta **57**

Statements of Ministers 57
2–7. The Six Teachers 65
Jīvaka Komārabhacca's Statement 67
Question on Fruits of Recluseship 71
The Six Outside Teachers and their Doctrines 76
First Two Visible Fruits 94
More Excellent Fruits 95
On Moral Discipline 102
Restraint of Sense Faculties (*Indriyasaṃvara*) 103
Mindfulness and Clear Comprehension (*Sati-sampajañña*) 104
Contentment (*Santosa*) 144
Abandoning Hindrances (*Nīvaraṇappahāna*) 149
The *Jhānas* 160
Insight Knowledge (*Vipassanā-ñāṇa*) 164
Knowledge of the Mind-made Body (*Manomay'iddhi-ñāṇa*) 169
Knowledge of Modes of Supernormal Power (*Iddhividha-ñāṇādi*) 170
Knowledge of Destruction of Cankers (*Āsavakkhaya-ñāṇa*) 171
Ajātasattu Declares Himself a Lay Follower 180
Going for Refuge (*Saraṇa-gamana*) 183

Translator's Preface

The present work is intended to make available an English translation of the *Sāmaññaphala Sutta* together with the doctrinally relevant material from the voluminous Pali commentarial literature that has accumulated around it. The *Sāmaññaphala Sutta*, The Discourse on the Fruits of Recluseship, is the second *sutta* in the entire Pali Canon and one of the most elevating of the Buddha's discourses. Immensely rich in content, the work is also a literary masterpiece distinguished by its chaste elegant diction and its beauty of poetic imagery. Against the backdrop of royal parricide and struggle for political power, on a beautiful full-moon night in autumn, when the rains have ceased and the water lilies bloom, the Buddha expounds the visible fruits of the recluse life, sketching the progress of the disciple from the first step of acquiring faith in the *Tathāgata*, the fully enlightened teacher, to its consummation in the destruction of the defilements and the realization of *Nibbāna*. Delivered in the last years of the Master's life, the *Sāmaññaphala Sutta* is a comprehensive summary of all that he had taught during his long ministry.

Because it offers the fullest canonical account of the spiritual training of the *bhikkhu* or Buddhist monk, the *Sāmaññaphala Sutta* has arrested the attention of the commentators, who have evolved an extensive body of literature dealing with the principal stages of the training expounded by the Buddha in the discourse. The primary commentary to the *Sāmaññaphala Sutta* is found in the *Sumaṅgalavilāsinī*, the complete commentary (*aṭṭhakathā*) to the *Dīgha Nikāya*. It is, of course, the work of the great Indian expositor Bhadantācariya Buddhaghosa, who based it on the ancient Sinhala commentaries that were entrusted to him by the *Saṅgha* resident at the Mahāvihāra in Sri Lanka in the fifth century C.E. The original subcommentary (*ṭīkā*) is ascribed to Ācariya Dhammapāla of Badaratittha, near Chennai, who probably lived in the sixth century. The purpose of the subcommentary is to clarify obscure points in the commentary, to explicate them further, and to elucidate matters in the *sutta* passed over by the commentary. Because Dhammapāla's subcommentary is often terse, a new subcommentary (*abhinavaṭīkā*) to the first part of the *Dīgha Nikāya* was composed in the late eighteenth century by the Burmese Sayadaw U Ñāṇābhivaṃsa. This work, the *Sādhuvilāsinī*, incorporates the contents of the old subcommentary, but elaborates upon them for the sake of greater clarity and adds numerous explanations of points in the commentary passed over by the old subcommentary.

The commentarial literature on the *Sāmaññaphala Sutta* could have been still more massive than it is if Buddhaghosa had chosen to comment at length on the *Jhānas* and kinds of direct knowledge. This, however, was not necessary. Because he had already treated these subjects in detail in the *Visuddhimagga*, he could pass over them lightly here and refer the reader to his *magnum opus* for a full account.

My standard in selecting material from the commentarial literature for inclusion in the present work is the same as that which guided my previous translations of *sutta-cum-*commentaries: to include everything I could from the exegetical works that is of fundamental doctrinal or practical importance, while omitting the less relevant digressions as well as the copious grammatical and etymological clarifications which have no meaning for an English reader. The attention of the reader is directed to the very substantial and instructive commentarial passages on clear comprehension, contentment, the abandonment of the hindrances, the destruction of the cankers, and the going for refuge. It is to be hoped that this material, like that included in my earlier works, will vindicate the commentaries against the criticisms of those who seize too readily upon their obvious shortcomings while turning a blind eye to their immense value as an aid in understanding and practising the *Dhamma*.

The format of this work is the same as that of my previous translations. The *sutta* is presented first without comment and with only a few notes needed for immediate clarification of the text. This is followed by the commentarial section, which has been composed in montage-like fashion drawing upon all three exegetical works to clarify the passage under discussion. The passages selected from the exegetical works have been arranged according to the numerical divisions of the *sutta*. Thus the explanation for any *sutta* statement elucidated in the commentaries can be located by consulting the commentarial section whose number corresponds to that of the *sutta* section. The comment on the statement is usually introduced by its key words set in capitals.

In rendering the title of the *sutta* and the word *samaṇa* I have followed the lead of previous translators in using the word "recluse". Though some translators have balked at this rendering, I feel that this choice is completely unobjectionable if it is pointed out that "recluse" here means simply one who has renounced the worldly life to undertake a full-time spiritual discipline and does not imply total isolation and a severing of all human ties.

In conclusion I would like to thank the Ven. Nyanaponika Mahāthera for his encouragement and counsel in this undertaking, and also for making available to me a selection of translated passages from the *Sāmaññaphala* commentaries he had prepared in the early 1950's. I would also like to thank Sister Ayyā Nyanasirī for patiently typing out the original manuscript of this work and for making some minor suggestions concerning style.

Bhikkhu Bodhi
Forest Hermitage
Kandy, Sri Lanka
May 1988

Texts Used

I. Primary Sources

Dīgha Nikāya: Sīlakkhandhavagga Pali. Burmese Buddhasāsana Council edition; Rangoon, 1954.

Dīgha Nikāya Aṭṭhakathā (*Sumaṅgalavilāsinī*)*: Sīlakkhandhavagga Aṭṭhakathā.* Burmese Buddhasāsana Council edition; Rangoon, 1956.

Dīgha Nikāya Ṭīkā: Sīlakkhandhavagga ṭīkā. Burmese Buddhasāsana Council edition; Rangoon, 1961.

Dīghanikāyaṭṭhakathā Ṭīka. Edited by Lily de Silva, Vol. I, London: Luzac and Co. Ltd., for the Pali Text Society, 1970.

Sīlakkhandhavagga Abhinavaṭīkā (*Sādhuvilāsinī*), by Ācarya Ñāṇābhivaṃsa Mahāthera. Burmese Buddhasāsana Council edition; Rangoon, 1961.

II. Previous Translations Consulted

Burma Pitaka Association. *Ten Dialogues from Dīgha Nikāya.* Rangoon, 1984. (Translation of the *sutta.*)

Nyanaponika Thera. *The Five Mental Hindrances.* BPS Wheel No. 26; new rev. ed., 1984. (Translation of *sutta* and commentarial passages on the abandoning of the five hindrances.)

Nyanaponika Thera. *The Threefold Refuge.* BPS Wheel No. 76; 1965. (Translation of commentarial passage on going for refuge.)

Rhys Davids, T.W. *Dialogues of the Buddha,* Part 1. Oxford University Press, 1899. (Translation of the *sutta.*)

Soma Thera. *The Way of Mindfulness: The Satipaṭṭhāna Sutta Commentary.* Fifth rev. ed., Kandy: BPS, 1981. (Translation of commentarial passage on mindfulness and clear comprehension.)

Walshe, Maurice. *Thus Have I Heard: The Long Discourses of the Buddha.* London: Wisdom Publications, 1987. (Translation of the *sutta.*)

List of Abbreviations

AN	*Aṅguttara Nikāya*
DN	*Dīgha Nikāya*
Dhp	*Dhammapada*
MN	*Majjhima Nikāya*
M-a	*Majjhima Nikāya Aṭṭhakathā* (BBC)
Nidd I	*Mahā Niddesa*
SN	*Saṃyutta Nikāya*
Sn	*Sutta Nipāta*
Vibh	*Vibhaṅga*
Vibh-a	*Vibhaṅga Aṭṭhakathā* (BBC)
Vism	*Visuddhimagga*
Vv	*Vimānavatthu*

All references are to the Pali Text Society editions, except for those texts above marked BBC, which refer to the Burmese Buddhasāsana Council editions. References to Vism are followed by the section and page number of *Bhikkhu* Ñāṇamoli's translation, *The Path of Purification*, 4th ed. (Kandy: BPS, 1979).

Introduction

The *Sāmaññaphala Sutta*, The Discourse on the Fruits of Recluseship, is the second *sutta* in the *Dīgha Nikāya*, The Collection of the Buddha's Long Discourses, which is itself the first of the five *Nikāyas* making up the *Sutta Piṭaka* of the Pali Canon. Although we have no demonstrable evidence that the compilers of the Canon arranged the *sutta*s in any deliberate pedagogical order, it seems almost certain that they assigned the *Sāmaññaphala Sutta* to the second place in the entire compilation of the Buddha's discourses in recognition of the momentous role it plays in establishing the fecundity of the Buddha's dispensation. Following immediately upon the *Brahmajāla Sutta*, the *Sāmaññaphala* fulfills a function for which its predecessor has only paved the way. If the *Brahmajāla* can be aptly described as the prolegomenon to the dispensation,[1] then the *Sāmaññaphala* might be described as the first and one of the pithiest statements of its substance. The primary project of the *Brahmajāla Sutta* was to clear away the conceptual and intellectual distortions that hinder the acquisition of right view, the first factor of the Noble Eightfold Path and thus the prerequisite for the successful development of the remaining path factors. The *Brahmajāla* attempted to achieve that aim by weaving a net of sixty-two categories capable of capturing all possible speculative views on the nature of the self and the world. By exposing these views as the cognitive hooks which craving uses to maintain its grip on the sentient organism with its six sense faculties, the *Brahmajāla* reveals the fruitlessness of all those philosophies and paths of life that are built upon an erroneous interpretation of the human situation.

---

1. See Bhikkhu Bodhi, *The Discourse on the All-Embracing Net of Views: The Brahmajāla Sutta and Its Commentaries* (Kandy: Buddhist Publication Society, 1978), p.1.

The *Sāmaññaphala Sutta* takes over precisely where the *Brahmajāla* leaves off, delivering the message which the former *sutta* could only adumbrate. Whereas the *Brahmajāla Sutta* has the negative task of pointing our the dangers and futility inherent in wrong views, the *Sāmaññaphala Sutta* sounds a triumphant and lyrical proclamation of the fruitfulness of the course of spiritual training founded upon right view. It is the Buddha's announcement to the world that the life of renunciation he adopted for himself, and opened up to humanity by founding the *Saṅgha*, brings immediately visible benefits in each of its stages. It is "good in the beginning" through the bliss of blamelessness that comes with the purification of conduct; "good in the middle" in yielding an exalted joy and bliss through the seclusion of the mind from the sensual hindrances; and "good in the end" because it culminates in the highest wisdom and peace through the transcending of all mundane bonds.

The *Sāmaññaphala Sutta* is the first of the Buddha's discourses in the textual order of the *Sutta Piṭaka* to make known the methodical step-by-step training that constitutes the heart of the practical *Dhamma*. In the Canon the Buddha himself is hailed for his unique role as discoverer and teacher of the path: "He is the arouser of the unarisen path, the producer of the unproduced path, the declarer of the undeclared path, the knower and seer of the path, the one skilled in the path" (MN 108/M III 8). By revealing this path in all its purity and perfection, the Buddha throws open to countless others "the doors to the Deathless," the way leading out from the suffering of repeated birth and death to the other shore of *Nibbāna*, where all rebirth and suffering cease. The *Sāmaññaphala Sutta* translates this path, stated in the abstract as the Noble Eightfold Path, into the terms of a concrete discipline. It presents the path, not as a mere list of factors and formulas, but as an ascending series of steps that rise up one upon the other, transforming the practitioner from a fickle worldling into a peerless spiritual conqueror victorious over all the defilements of mind.

In the terminology of the texts, this methodical discipline is called "the gradual training" (*anupubbasikkhā*). The

Sāmaññaphala Sutta discloses that gradual training, as it was envisaged and expounded by the Buddha himself, in as comprehensive a form as can be found anywhere in the Pali Canon. Having made its first canonical appearance in the *Sāmaññaphala*, the same gradual training is reiterated time and again, with only minor variations, throughout the *Sutta Piṭaka*. In the *Dīgha Nikāya* alone the basic schematism set forth in the *Sāmaññaphala* runs like a red thread through almost all the following *sutta*s in the first volume, the formulation alone being modified to suit the context. Thus in the *Ambaṭṭha Sutta* (DN 3) the steps of the gradual training are used to explain the twin virtues of knowledge (*vijjā*) and conduct (*caraṇa*), which makes a person "best of gods and men." In the *Soṇadaṇḍa Sutta* (DN 4) the same steps are distributed into the two categories of morality (*sīla*) and wisdom (*paññā*), the characteristics of the genuine brahmin. In the *Mahāsīhanāda Sutta* (DN 8) the training is divided into the threefold accomplishment: in morality, mastery of mind, and wisdom; and again in the *Subha Sutta* (DN 10) it is divided into noble morality, noble concentration, and noble wisdom. In the other *Nikāyas*, particularly the *Majjhima*, the gradual training reappears numerous times, though always in a more compressed version than in the *Dīgha*. And in the narrative of the Buddha's last days, the *Mahāparinibbāna Sutta* (DN 16), when it is stated so often that the Exalted One instructed the monks in morality, concentration, and wisdom, we can be sure that his sermons would have dealt with the same sequence of steps explained in detail in the *Sāmaññaphala Sutta*.

The title of the discourse already suggests that the work will be a vindication of the special mode of life the Buddha elected to follow and for which he served as the supreme exemplar—the life of a *bhikkhu*, a mendicant monk. The word *sāmañña* is an abstract noun formed from *samaṇa*, here rendered "recluse," derived from a root meaning "to strive." The word *samaṇa* originally seems to have been applied to those religious seekers, numerous in ancient India, who devoted themselves to the practice of austerities and stringent asceticism as the main endeavour of their discipline. However, by the Buddha's time the term came to be applied indiscriminately to all those outside the fold of orthodox Brahmanism who led a homeless life on vaguely spiritual grounds. It included ascetics who engaged in the most grueling exercises of self-mortification as well as freely moving wanderers who saw nothing wrong in the tender touch of their female companions (see MN 45/M I 305); it included skeptics and atheists, mystics and rationalists, and proponents of systems of belief bewildering in their sheer diversity. Roaming the rural countryside of northern India or sequestered in its jungles, debating with each other in halls built especially for that purpose or preaching to the village folk who supported them with alms, the *samaṇas* constituted a distinct class of Indian society outside the tightly class-bound structure of that society. Their very presence, whether visible or invisible, held out a promise to those disillusioned with the pleasures of secular life and a question mark to those comfortably entrenched within it.

The Buddha too was a *samaṇa*, known to his contemporaries as "the recluse Gotama," and his *bhikkhu* disciples were also *samaṇas*, distinguished from others with a similar demeanour and lifestyle as "the recluses who follow the son of the Sakyan clan." Originating in response to a question whether the life of a recluse is capable of yielding fruits that are visible here and now, the *Sāmaññaphala Sutta* is intended to explain to the secular world at large why so many "young men of good family" (and women as well) chose to leave behind their homes, wealth, loved ones, and status in order to follow the Sage of the Sakyan clan into homelessness. For those comfortably adjusted to their accustomed routines, the homeless life of renunciation, self-restraint, striving, and solitary meditation poses an impenetrable enigma. And the enigma remains impenetrable so long as the benefits that such a way of life can yield have not been clearly demonstrated. The Buddha's discourse aims at dispelling the perplexities the people of the world may face when encountering the life of homelessness by showing that this life can reward those who lead it in earnest with fruits that are concrete, personal, and directly verifiable.

The question put to the Buddha on that lovely full-moon night in the quiet of the Mango Grove—Is it possible to point out any visible fruits of the recluse life?—has a significance that goes far beyond the particular circumstances under which it was uttered. The question indicates a recognition, however vague, of an element of inadequacy underlying mundane life. It also shows a tentative probing into the possibility of a deeper level of fulfillment. The Buddha's reply, reverberating down the centuries, informs us not only that the life of a recluse is abundantly fruitful, but also reveals that the fruits of the renunciant life, when pursued in accordance with the true *Dhamma*, are of a qualitatively different order than the enjoyments of secular life. While the latter are transient, tied up with desire and clinging, and issue in sorrow when expectations fail, the fruits of recluseship lead out of the restlessness of desire and alone can quench our thirst for a peace and happiness that are inviolable.

The Setting of the Discourse

The *Sāmaññaphala Sutta* was addressed by the Buddha to King Ajātasattu, ruler of the powerful middle Indian state of Magadha, which had already embarked on the course of conquest and absorption of neighbouring states that was to make it the nucleus of the first major Indian empire. The historical background to the discourse is only barely suggested by the preamble to the *sutta*, but is sketched for us by the commentary: the story of how Ajātasattu fell under the evil influence of Devadatta, seized the throne from his father, the righteous King Bimbisāra, had his father imprisoned and murdered, and was subsequently tormented by remorse. A knowledge of that story, though not essential to understanding the discourse, heightens and deepens the atmosphere in which the *sutta* unfolds. Contemplated in juxtaposition, the Buddha's discourse and the historical background create between them a particularly poignant dramatic tension: on the one side, the life of renunciation, moral purity, solitude, and contemplation extolled by the Buddha; on the other, the lawless greed for power that led Ajātasattu to parricide and the throne, the pangs of guilt and remorse that shattered his sleep, and the yearning for peace that induced him to visit the Exalted One dwelling in the Mango Grove.

The *Sāmaññaphala Sutta* must have been spoken by the Buddha during the very last years of his life. When surveying the calm and quiet community of *bhikkhus*, Ajātasattu utters an exclamation mentioning his son Udāyibhadda, and this gives us a clue for narrowing down the occasion of the discourse. According to the commentaries, it was in the thirty-seventh year after the Enlightenment, when the Buddha was seventy-two years old, that Devadatta commenced his drive to gain leadership of the *Saṅgha*. Thus it must have been in the same year that Ajātasattu usurped the throne. Following his accession to power, Ajātasattu launched an extended war against his uncle, King Pasenadi of Kosala, which ended with a truce sealed by the gift in marriage of Pasenadi's daughter, Princess Vajirā. It was from this union that the boy Udāyibhadda was born. Thus, if we allow at least three years for Ajātasattu to have conducted his war, married Vajirā, and sired his son, this would place the *Sāmaññaphala Sutta* somewhere in the last five years of the Buddha's life.

The Six Teachers

Before answering Ajātasattu's question on the fruits of recluseship, the Buddha asks him whether he has previously ever approached any other recluses or brahmins with this question. The king answers in the affirmative, and his account of his meeting with six other religious teachers provides the opportunity for a short survey of the types of philosophical doctrines which were being promulgated by the wandering ascetic teachers of the Ganges valley during the fifth and sixth centuries B.C. This section of the *sutta* is almost certainly a literary fabrication devised by the compilers of the Canon for polemical purposes. It may be regarded as an extension, from a different angle, of the project undertaken by the *Brahmajāla Sutta*—a survey of the variety of wrong views. But whereas the *Brahmajāla* aims at exhaustiveness and presents its survey under the rubric of speculations about the self and the world, the *Sāmaññaphala* sets itself a more modest aim: it is concerned only with the views in circulation among the Buddha's contemporaries, and rather than subjecting them to some categorical scheme, it states them in the terms in which their proponents formulated them.

The six teachers whose views are recounted by King Ajātasattu are frequently referred to as a group in the Pali Canon, though there is no evidence that the Buddha ever met with any of them face to face. They all seem to have been senior to the Buddha, and from the stock description of them as leaders of orders and groups, etc. (§2–7) they must have been influential and highly venerated in their day. Western scholars have come to designate them as "the six heretics," though as they make no profession to adhere either to Buddhism or Brahmanism they cannot be considered as heretics within the Buddhist or Brahmanic fold. Thus it would be more accurate to speak of them as the six outside teachers. Their views all fall outside the wide perimeters of orthodox Brahmanism and are indicative of the intellectual ferment that had come to the fore as part of the reaction against Brahmanic orthodoxy during the Buddha's age.

Though the statements ascribed to the six teachers by the *Sāmaññaphala Sutta* must doubtlessly contain formulations that were part of their established creeds, it is also likely that the formulas became garbled and confused in the course of oral transmission. Apart from the Buddhist scriptures, there is no other information at all on the views of four of the teachers. The Jaina scriptures provide information of the views of Makkhali Gosāla and Nigaṇṭha Nātaputta, the historical founder of Jainism, and this source confirms the *Sāmaññaphala* as being substantially correct in its representation of Makkhali's views, though not those of Nigaṇṭha Nātaputta.[2] The information in the commentaries

2. Jacobi points out that the teaching ascribed to Nigaṇṭha Nātaputta, while not an accurate description of the Jaina creed, contains nothing alien to it: Introduction to *Jaina Sutras*, Pt.2, Sacred Books of the East, Vol. 45 (Oxford, 1895), pp. xx–xxi.

especially must be treated with a great deal of caution. The short biographical sketches of the outside teachers are almost certainly contrived for the sake of denigration. While it is plausible that the commentaries have preserved some ancient material elucidating their old rivals' creeds, it often appears that the commentators are engaging in guesswork or straining their interpretations to exhibit the Buddha's opponents in an excessively unfavourable light.

Although the details of the six teachers' doctrines may be obscure, on the basis of the *Sāmaññaphala Sutta* it is possible to discern the general characteristics of each view. Pūraṇa Kassapa, whose name regularly heads the list of the six, was a proponent of the doctrine of the inefficacy of action (*akiriya-vāda*). As expounded in the *sutta*, this view denies that volitional actions are capable of bearing fruit, and as a consequence leads to the rejection of the validity of moral judgements and distinctions. On first consideration this view seems to be a variant on the materialistic annihilationism of Ajita Kesakambala. However, there are indications elsewhere in the Canon that Pūraṇa's teachings had close connections with the creed of Makkhali Gosāla, and thus his moral antinomianism would follow not from materialistic premises, but from a doctrine of hardline determinism.[3]

Makkhali Gosāla, who was an early associate of the Jain teacher Nigaṇṭha Nātaputta before the two went their separate ways, was the leader of the religious sect called the Ājīvikas, which survived in India until medieval times before vanishing completely from the Indian scene.[4] The main tenet of Makkhali's

3. At AN 6:57/III 388-84 Makkhali's doctrine of the six classes of men is ascribed to Pūraṇa Kassapa, who assigns Makkhali himself to the highest class. And at SN 22:60/III 69 and SN 46:56/V126 the denial of causes and conditions is ascribed to Pūraṇa in exactly the same way the doctrine is enunciated by Makkhali.

4. A full study of this school of Indian thought is A.L. Basham, *History and Doctrines of the Ājīvikas* (1951; reprinted, Delhi: Motilal Banarsidass, 1981). Chapters XII and XIII give a detailed account of Makkhali Gosāla's philosophy.

philosophy was the belief that the entire cosmic process is rigidly controlled by a principle called *niyati*, destiny or fate. Destiny holds everything within its grip. Under its control every soul has to pass through a fixed course in *saṃsāra* before attaining release. Human effort and volition are utterly powerless to alter this course, and thus the wise by diligent effort cannot shorten their bondage to the round of rebirths, nor do the foolish by their negligence lengthen it. Makkhali's system also involved a fantastically elaborate cosmology, the key concepts of which are enumerated in his statement. It seems that this was not a simple list of the contents of the universe, but a map of the states through which the soul must pass in its course of transmigration before it could gain emancipation.

Ajita Kesakambala's doctrine was a straightforward materialism which maintained that the person is essentially identical with his body. The breaking up of the body at death thus entails the utter annihilation of the person, without any principle of conscious continuity beyond the grave or moral retribution for deeds. Pakudha Kaccāyana advocates, in contrast, an atomism which recognized, in addition to the material components of the person, an indestructible individual soul. Pakudha deduced, from the imperishable nature of the soul, conclusions that spurned the very basis of morality: since the soul cannot be injured or destroyed, even the notion of killing becomes untenable.

Nigaṇṭha Nātaputta is identical with Vardhamāna Mahāvīra, the historical founder of Jainism, though regarded within his own tradition as the most recent of a long line of *tīrthaṅkaras* or "ford-makers." The obscure statement by which he is represented in *Sāmaññaphala Sutta* has not been traced to the Jaina scriptures, but a conjecture can be offered why more typical views of his stated in other Pali *sutta*s (e.g. MN 14, MN 101) have not been brought in here. Since the Jaina leader affirmed the fruitfulness of the recluse life and claimed that his discipline brings an end to suffering—though through doctrines and practices rejected by the Buddha—to have introduced these views here would have required divergence from the forward movement of the *sutta*. The last of the six teachers, Sañjaya Belaṭṭhaputta, was a skeptic.

In the *Brahmajāla Sutta* his position is included among the "endless equivocators" or "eel-wrigglers" who are incapable of taking a definite stance on the vital philosophical questions of the day.

Elsewhere in the Pali Canon the Buddha has exposed the debacle to which these views must lead, but in the *Sāmaññaphala Sutta* he does not speak a word against them. He simply leaves it to King Ajātasattu to declare his own dissatisfaction with their proponents, who must have displeased him not only by their failure to answer his question on the fruits of recluseship, but also because their doctrines were incapable of offering him any outlet from the crisis brought on by his conscience.

The Fruits of Recluseship

When he has finished telling the Buddha about his meetings with the six outside teachers, King Ajātasattu repeats his original question, and this time the Buddha accepts it and undertakes to explain the visible fruits of recluseship. In the technical terminology of the *Dhamma* the expression "fruits of recluseship" is used to signify the four stages of sanctity that follow upon the attainment of the corresponding supramundane paths. These are the fruits of stream-entry, once-returning, non-returning, and *arahatship* (see SN 45:35 /v. 25). In the *Sāmaññaphala Sutta*, however, the Buddha does not employ the term in this more technical sense, which at this point would hardly have been intelligible to the king, but uses it instead to indicate the concrete experiential benefits that may be attained by those who adopt the homeless life.

Altogether the Buddha will point out *fourteen fruits of recluseship*, which unfold in a generally ascending scale of value. The first two he describes have a tangible, temporal, extrinsic character. They are thus well-suited for the understanding of a man like Ajātasattu, already disposed to evaluate things from the standpoint of expediency and personal advantage. The first is the case of a palace slave (§34) who by becoming a monk is no longer obliged to obey the king, but on the contrary is entitled to receive from his former master, the ruler of the land, homage, cordial treatment, and material offerings. The second case (§37) is that of a householder who by becoming a monk is no longer obliged to pay taxes and serve the state, but again merits the king's veneration. Both these fruits of recluseship, it should be pointed out, would accrue to those who went forth into homelessness in any religious order that maintained the basic standards of virtuous conduct. They are not the exclusive prerogatives of members of the Buddhist order.

While these two fruits of recluseship must have shaken the king's complacency regarding the absoluteness of his own power and authority—and in this respect they served as a highly effective teaching device—they could hardly have given him full satisfaction. Confronted with the Buddha Gotama, a man of the *khattiya* class and of royal blood like himself, who had renounced the privileges of royalty for a life of mendicancy, and confronted with a community of *bhikkhus* that included many former brahmins and high-ranking nobles, he would have realized that these "sons of good family" had gone forth into homelessness with some higher objective in view than refuge from slavery and taxation. Thus he asks the Buddha to point out other visible fruits of recluseship "more excellent and sublime" than the previous two fruits. In reply the Buddha sets out to expound the gradual training, which leads by stages to the superior fruits of the homeless life that are the precious treasures of his dispensation.

The *twelve higher fruits of recluseship* are the four *Jhānas* and the eight cognitive achievements collected under the umbrella term *vijjā*, clear knowledge. Before he can reveal these fruits of homelessness, however, in order to make sure that their value and significance are properly appreciated, the Buddha must explain the causal basis for their attainment. Thus he starts his exposition by describing the course of training that culminates in the fruits of recluseship—the seeds, roots, trunks, and branches that must be properly nurtured for the homeless life to yield a successful harvest.

The entire sequence of steps starts with the arising of a *Tathāgata*, a perfectly enlightened Buddha, as the indispensable condition for the complete gamut of the fruits of recluseship being made accessible to the world (§41). It has been pointed out often enough that the four *Jhānas* and six of the higher knowledges (the first and last being excepted) are not exclusive to the Buddha's dispensation, but can be reached by contemplatives following other spiritual disciplines as well. Although this is true it must also be said that the sequence of steps that issues in the higher attainments has nowhere else been described so methodically and with such attention to the inner dynamics of spiritual transformation as by the Buddha, while the deployment of the entire sequence as a means to attain deliverance from suffering is unique to the Buddha's dispensation. Thus, even if we recognize the above caveat, the *sutta* is well justified in making the arising of a Buddha the precondition for the twelve "more excellent and sublime" fruits of recluseship.

The response to the Buddha's exposition of the *Dhamma*, and the first step along the path, is the gaining of faith in the *Tathāgata*. The gaining of faith leads to the going forth into homelessness (§42-43). Though the Buddha taught the *Dhamma* extensively to both his ordained and lay disciples and declared that householders are fully capable of attaining the first three stages of sanctity, he also makes it plain that the homeless life is the mode of living most conducive to reaching the complete end of suffering without delay or hindrance. For it is in the homeless life that all the distractions of the world and the pressures of secular duties are held at bay and the most adequate outer conditions are established for the internal work of self-purification. It is for this reason that the Buddha takes the going forth into homelessness as the starting point of his exposition and treats it as the basis for all further development along the path.

The first stage of the gradual training following the entrance into homelessness is the training in moral discipline (*sīla*). The moral precepts laid down in the *Pātimokkha*, the *bhikkhu's* code of discipline, and more extensively in the *Vinaya*, have the purpose of enabling the practitioner to gain control over his bodily and verbal actions and thereby debilitate their roots in the unwholesome tendencies of the mind. The *Sāmaññaphala Sutta* presents an elaborately detailed analysis of the moral training of the monk, divided into three sections, the first (§45) common to the explanation of the gradual training in the *Majjhima Nikāya*, the second and third (§46–62) peculiar to the *Dīgha Nikāya* version. This is of interest not only in showing the standards of conduct to which the *bhikkhu* is expected to conform, but also in revealing the kinds of activity and modes of livelihood indulged in by recluses and brahmins contemporary with the Buddha.

The steps that follow moral discipline involve a progressive internalization of the process of self-mastery initiated by the undertaking of the moral precepts. By the practice of restraint of the sense faculties (*indriyasaṃvara*, §64) the disciple learns to control not merely his active responses to the data of the senses, but the mind's deeply ingrained tendencies to fasten upon the agreeable and disagreeable qualities of things as nutriment for its dispositions to greed and aversion. This endeavour to master the workings of the mind is pursued still further by the practice of mindfulness and clear comprehension (*sati-sampajañña*, §65), which aims at bringing all the innumerable activities of everyday life into the clear light of awareness and at penetrating through to an understanding of their essential nature.

The commentary to this section offers an extremely valuable detailed explanation of the practice of clear comprehension. It divides this practice into four aspects, illustrating the third aspect, clear comprehension of the domain of meditation, with stories about the methods of meditation practice undertaken by the ancient monks of Sri Lanka. The commentary and subcommentaries together present an extensive account of the fourth aspect of clear comprehension—clear comprehension as non-delusion—bringing in the *Abhidhamma* analysis of *dhammas* to show how all the diverse activities mentioned in the *sutta* passage are to be understood, not as the actions of a self-sufficient agent, but as bare activities fully explicable in terms of conditionally interrelated sequences of bodily and mental events free from the directorship of an ego. The factor of contentment (*santosa*, §66) completes the preparatory training of the *bhikkhu* by nurturing such qualities essential to his quest for liberation as fewness of wants, simplicity, ease of support, patience, and vigour.

The preliminary steps of moral discipline, restraint of the sense faculties, mindfulness and clear comprehension, and contentment are called by the commentary the "four requisites" for one who aims at reaching the higher fruits of recluseship. When they have been sufficiently well developed to provide a secure basis for living in solitude, the *bhikkhu* resorts to a secluded dwelling where he can apply himself in full earnestness to his meditation practice. The primary task in the initial phase of intensive meditation is the abandoning of the five hindrances, called by the Buddha the five defilements of mind which obstruct concentration and weaken wisdom. The Buddha illustrates the abandoning of the hindrances with five striking similes, elaborated upon even further by the commentary (§67–75).

According to the *sutta*'s own pronouncements the higher fruits of recluseship begin only with the first *Jhāna*. However, the *sutta* also makes it plain that each of the preparatory stages leading up to the *Jhānas* brings along its own directly experienced benefit. Thus the training in moral discipline provides the *bhikkhu* with a sense of security from moral danger, enabling him to experience within himself a blameless happiness (*anavajja-sukha*). The restraining of the sense faculties issues in a happiness that cannot be blemished by greed and aversion (*abyāseka-sukha*). Mindfulness and clear comprehension enfold all activities in an envelope of lucid awareness and give the practitioner a self-possession that protects the growing germ of inward calm. Contentment enables him to move about freely like a bird on the wing. And with the abandoning of the hindrances, gladness arises, leading by stages to rapture, tranquillity, happiness, and deepened concentration (§76).[5]

The deepened concentration that results from the removal of the hindrances, developed and cultivated, brings the attainment of the first *Jhāna*, which is the first of the "more excellent" fruits of recluseship. As each *Jhāna* is in turn mastered and transcended, it issues in the attainment of the following *Jhānas*, each of which is

5. The relevant Pali noun terms are: *pāmojja*, *pīti*, *passaddhi*, *sukha*, *samādhi*.

described as a fruit of recluseship "more excellent and sublime" than the ones which preceded it (§77–84). Although the *Jhānas* are still mundane achievements, not exclusive to the Buddha's dispensation and no sure guarantee of enlightenment, the fact that the Buddha invariably includes them in the gradual training indicates that they should not be lightly dismissed as states of mere euphoric intoxication leading astray from the path. Even if they are not indispensable for reaching the supramundane paths and fruits, they are extolled and encouraged by the Buddha as providing a foretaste here and now of the bliss of *Nibbāna* and as a powerful instrument for securing the base of calm concentration conducive to the arising of the higher wisdom.

The Buddha illustrates each of the four *Jhānas* with a simile of astounding beauty that captures the distinct nuance of its experiential quality. This string of similes—continuing on into the subsequent fruits of recluseship—translates the exalted states of spiritual experience described by the *sutta* into the familiar images of daily life. The richness and suggestive beauty of these similes raise the ambiance of the *Sāmaññaphala Sutta* to the high pitch of joyful inspiration and triumphant exultation from which they issue forth.

The most direct path to deliverance proceeds without interval from the *Jhānas* to the development of insight and the attainment of the supramundane paths. However, in this *sutta* the Buddha wishes to give an extensive exposition covering all the exalted benefits that may be achieved in the life of homelessness. Therefore, instead of treating the stage of wisdom exclusively in terms of insight and the supramundane paths, he uses it as a rubric for introducing a variety of higher types of knowledge attainable by one with mastery over the four *Jhānas*. These types of knowledge, eight in number, contain as their core a set of six known as the modes of direct knowledge (*abhiññā*). These are frequently mentioned together in the *sutta*s and held up as objectives of the Buddhist spiritual training. To this set two others are added, less often mentioned under their own names, but here made to precede the more familiar set. The first of these is insight knowledge (*vipassanā-ñāṇa*). In more condensed presentations of the teaching this factor is implicitly comprised in the sixth and final direct knowledge, as the practice instrumental in effecting the destruction of the cankers. Here, however, it is extracted and treated as a type of knowledge in its own right and the first of the fruits of recluseship belonging to the stage of wisdom (§85–86).

The knowledge of the mind-made body (§87–88), a supernormal power of drawing out the subtle psychic body from its gross material envelope, is also introduced as a separate fruit of recluseship before the Buddha presents his standard exposition of the six modes of direct knowledge (§89–98). The entire disquisition on the fruits of recluseship is then brought to its climax with the knowledge of the destruction of the cankers (§99–100). This is the path of *arahatship* issuing in the fruit of *arahatship*, the liberation of mind and liberation by wisdom attained when the cankers have been fully destroyed. With this we reach the final goal of the Buddha's teaching, and the fruit of recluseship for which all the others have prepared the way and find the reason for their inclusion in the training. Thus the Buddha concludes his discourse by stating that "there is no other fruit of recluseship higher or more sublime than this one."

Following the discourse, the *sutta* returns to the personal drama out of which it arose. Deeply moved, King Ajātasattu applauds the Buddha's presentation of the *Dhamma* and then declares himself a lay follower of the Buddha by going for refuge in the Triple Gem. This response provides the commentary with an opportunity for inserting a compact little essay that explores the wide-ranging significance of the going for refuge, that decisive first step by which one enters the Buddhist path.

The king then confesses to the Buddha his crime of killing his father, the Buddha's devoted patron, a confession the Buddha acknowledges for the sake of the king's future restraint. When Ajātasattu has left, the Buddha explains to the *bhikkhus* that if the king had not slain his father, while sitting there listening to the discourse, he would have opened the eye of *Dhamma* and attained the stage of a stream-enterer. But Ajātasattu had a different destiny to follow. The records indicate that despite his conversion he continued his expansionist policy until he was eventually slain by his own beloved son Udāyibhadda. As a consequence of committing parricide, the commentary tells us, he was reborn in hell, but in a distant future life he will achieve the enlightenment of a *paccekabuddha* and attain final *Nibbāna*.

Part One

The Text of the Sāmaññaphala Sutta

Statements of the Ministers

1. Thus have I heard. On one occasion the Exalted One was dwelling at Rājagaha, in Jīvaka Komārabhacca's Mango Grove, together with a large company of twelve hundred and fifty *bhikkhus*. At the time, on the fifteenth-day Uposatha, the full-moon night of Komudī in the fourth month,[6] King Ajātasattu of Magadha, the son of Queen Videha, was sitting on the upper terrace of his palace surrounded by his ministers. There the king uttered the following joyful exclamation:

"How delightful, friends, is this moonlit night! How beautiful is this moonlit night! How lovely is this moonlit night! How tranquil is this moonlit night! How auspicious is this moonlit night! Is there any recluse or brahmin that we could visit tonight who might be able to bring peace to my mind?"

2. Thereupon one of his ministers said: "Your majesty, there is Pūraṇa Kassapa, the leader of an order, the leader of a group, the teacher of a group, well-known and famous, a spiritual leader whom many people esteem as holy. He is aged, long gone forth, advanced in years, in the last phase of life. Your majesty should visit him. Perhaps he might bring peace to your mind." But when this was said, King Ajātasattu remained silent.

3–7. Other ministers said: "Your majesty, there is Makkhali Gosāla … Ajita Kesakambala … Pakudha Kaccāyana … Sañjaya Belaṭṭhaputta … Nigaṇṭha Nātaputta, the leader of an order, the leader of a group, the teacher of a group, well-known and famous,

---

6. This would be the month of Kattika (October–November). The full-moon night of this month is called Komudi because it is said to be the time when the white water lily (*kumuda*) blooms.

a spiritual leader whom many people esteem as holy. He is aged, long gone forth, advanced in years, in the last phase of life. Your majesty should visit him. Perhaps he might bring peace to your mind." But when this was said, King Ajātasattu remained silent.

The Statement of Jīvaka Komārabhacca

8. All this time Jīvaka Komārabhacca sat silently not far from King Ajātasattu. The king then said to him: "Friend Jīvaka, why do you keep silent?"

Jīvaka said: "Your majesty, the Exalted One, the Worthy One, the perfectly enlightened Buddha, together with a large company of twelve hundred and fifty *bhikkhus*, is now dwelling in our Mango Grove. A favourable report concerning him is circulating thus: 'This Exalted One is a worthy one, perfectly enlightened, endowed with clear knowledge and conduct, accomplished, a knower of the world, unsurpassed trainer of men to be tamed, teacher of gods and men, enlightened and exalted.' Your majesty should visit the Exalted One. Perhaps if you visit him he might bring peace to your mind."

9. "Then get the elephant vehicles prepared, friend Jīvaka."

"Yes, your majesty!" Jīvaka replied. He then had five hundred female elephants prepared, as well as the king's personal bull-elephant, and announced to the king: "Your majesty, your elephant vehicles are ready. Do as you think fit."

10. King Ajātasattu then had five hundred of his women mounted on the female elephants, one on each, while he himself mounted his personal bull-elephant. With his attendants carrying torches, he went forth from Rājagaha in full royal splendour, setting out in the direction of Jīvaka's Mango Grove.

When King Ajātasattu was not far from the Mango Grove, he was suddenly gripped by fear, trepidation, and terror. Frightened, agitated, and terror-stricken, he said to Jīvaka: "You aren't deceiving me, are you, friend Jīvaka? You aren't betraying me? You aren't about to turn me over to my enemies? How could there be such a large company of *bhikkhus*, twelve hundred and fifty *bhikkhus*, without any sound of sneezing or coughing, or any noise at all?"

"Do not be afraid, great king. Do not be afraid. I am not deceiving you, your majesty, or betraying you, or turning you over to your enemies. Go forward, great king! Go straight forward! Those are lamps burning in the pavilion hall."

The Question on the Fruits of Recluseship

11. Then King Ajātasattu, having gone by elephant as far as he could, dismounted and approached the door of the pavilion hall on foot. Having approached, he asked Jīvaka: "But where, Jīvaka, is the Exalted One?"

"That is the Exalted One, great king. He is the one sitting against the middle pillar, facing east, in front of the company of *bhikkhus*."

12. King Ajātasattu then approached the Exalted One and stood to one side. As he stood there surveying the company of *bhikkhus*, which sat in complete silence as serene as a calm lake, he uttered the following joyful exclamation: "May my son, the Prince Udāyibhadda, enjoy such peace as the company of *bhikkhus* now enjoys!"

(The Exalted One said:) "Do your thoughts, great king, follow the call of your affection?"

"Venerable sir, I love my son, the Prince Udāyibhadda. May he enjoy such peace as the company of *bhikkhus* now enjoys."

13. King Ajātasattu then paid homage to the Exalted One, reverently saluted the company of *bhikkhus*, sat down to one side, and said to the Exalted One: "Venerable sir, I would like to ask the Exalted One about a certain point, if he would take the time to answer my question."

"Ask whatever you wish to, great king."

14. "There are, venerable sir, various crafts, such as elephant trainers, horse trainers, charioteers, archers, standard bearers, camp marshals, commandos, high royal officers, front-line soldiers, bull-warriors, military heroes, mail-clad warriors, domestic slaves, confectioners, barbers, bath attendants, cooks, garland-makers, laundrymen, weavers, basketmakers, potters, statisticians, accountants, and various other crafts of a similar nature.

All those (who practise these crafts) enjoy here and now the visible fruits of their crafts. They obtain happiness and joy themselves, and they give happiness and joy to their parents, wives and children, and their friends and colleagues. They establish an excellent presentation of gifts to recluses and brahmins—leading to heaven, ripening in happiness, conducing to a heavenly rebirth. Is it possible, venerable sir, to point out any fruit of recluseship that is similarly visible here and now?"

15. "Do you remember, great king, ever asking other recluses and brahmins this question?"

"I do remember asking them, venerable sir."

"If it isn't troublesome for you, please tell us how they answered."

"It is not troublesome for me, venerable sir, when the Exalted One or anyone like him is present."

"Then speak, great king."

The Doctrine of Pūraṇa Kassapa

16. "One time, I approached Pūraṇa Kassapa, exchanged greetings and courtesies with him, and sat down to one side. I then asked him (*as in* §14) if he could point out any fruit of recluseship visible here and now.

17. "When I had finished speaking, Pūraṇa Kassapa said to me: 'Great king, if one acts or induces others to act, mutilates or induces others to mutilate, tortures or induces others to torture, inflicts sorrow or induces others to inflict sorrow, oppresses or induces others to oppress, intimidates or induces others to intimidate; if one destroys life, takes what is not given, breaks into houses, plunders wealth, commits burglary, ambushes highways, commits adultery, speaks falsehood—one does no evil. If with a razor-edged disk one were to reduce all the living beings on this earth to a single heap and pile of flesh, by doing so there would be no evil or outcome of evil. If one were to go along the south bank of the Ganges killing and inducing others to kill, mutilating and inducing others to mutilate, torturing and inducing others to torture, by doing so there would be no evil or outcome of evil. If

one were to go along the north bank of the Ganges giving gifts and inducing others to give gifts, making offerings and inducing others to make offerings, by doing so there would be no merit or outcome of merit. By giving, self-control, restraint, and truthful speech there is no merit or outcome of merit.'

"Thus, venerable sir, when I asked Pūraṇa Kassapa about a visible fruit of recluseship, he explained to me (his doctrine of) the inefficacy of action. Venerable sir, just as if one asked about a mango would speak about a breadfruit, or as if one asked about a breadfruit would speak about a mango, in the same way when I asked Pūraṇa Kassapa about a visible fruit of recluseship he explained to me (his doctrine of) the inefficacy of action. Then, venerable sir, I thought to myself: 'One like myself should not think of troubling a recluse or brahmin living in his realm.' So I neither rejoiced in the statement of Pūraṇa Kassapa nor did I reject it. But, though I neither rejoiced in it nor rejected it, I still felt dissatisfied, yet did not utter a word of dissatisfaction. Without accepting his doctrine, without embracing it, I got up from my seat and left.

The Doctrine of Makkhali Gosāla

18. "Another time, venerable sir, I approached Makkhali Gosāla, exchanged greetings and courtesies with him, and sat down to one side. I then asked him (*as in* §14) if he could point out a fruit of recluseship visible here and now.

19. "When I had finished speaking, Makkhali Gosāla said to me: 'Great king, there is no cause or condition for the defilement of beings; beings are defiled without any cause or condition. There is no cause or condition for the purification of beings; beings are purified without cause or condition. There is no self-determination, no determination by others, no personal determination. There is no power, no energy, no personal strength, no personal fortitude. All sentient beings, all living beings, all creatures, all souls, are helpless, powerless, devoid of energy. Undergoing transformation by destiny, circumstance, and nature, they experience pleasure and pain in the six classes of men.

'There are fourteen hundred thousand principal modes of origin (for living beings) and six thousand (others) and six hundred (others). There are five hundred kinds of *kamma* and five kinds of *kamma* and three kinds of *kamma* and full *kamma* and half-*kamma*. There are sixty-two pathways, sixty-two sub-aeons, six classes of men, eight stages in the life of man, forty-nine hundred modes of livelihood, forty-nine hundred kinds of wanderers, forty-nine hundred abodes of *Nāgas*,[7] two thousand faculties, three thousand hells, thirty-six realms of dust, seven spheres of percipient beings, seven spheres of non-percipient beings, seven kinds of jointed plants, seven kinds of gods, seven kinds of human beings, seven kinds of demons, seven great lakes, seven major kinds of knots, seven hundred minor kinds of knots, seven major precipices, seven hundred minor precipices, seven major kinds of dreams, seven hundred minor kinds of dreams, eighty-four hundred thousand great aeons. The foolish and the wise, having roamed and wandered through these, will alike make an end to suffering.

'Though one might think: "By this moral discipline or observance or austerity or holy life I will ripen unripened *kamma* and eliminate ripened *kamma* whenever it comes up"—that cannot be. For pleasure and pain are measured out. *Saṃsāra*'s limits are fixed, and they can neither be shortened nor extended. There is no advancing forward and no falling back. Just as, when a ball of string is thrown, it rolls along unwinding until it comes to its end, in the same way, the foolish and the wise roam and wander (for the fixed length of time), after which they make an end to suffering.'

20. "Thus, venerable sir, when I asked Makkhali Gosāla about a visible fruit of recluseship, he explained to me (his doctrine of) purification through wandering in *saṃsāra*. Venerable sir, just as if one asked about a mango would speak about a breadfruit, or as if one asked about a breadfruit would speak about a mango, in the same way, when I asked Makkhali Gosāla about a visible fruit

7. *Nāga*: a dragon-like being in Indian mythology, supposed to dwell in the sea or beneath the earth.

of recluseship, he explained to me (his doctrine of) purification through wandering in *saṃsāra*. Then, venerable sir, I thought to myself: 'One like myself should not think of troubling a recluse or brahmin living in his realm.' So I neither rejoiced in the statement of Makkhali Gosāla nor did I reject it. But, though I neither rejoiced in it nor rejected it, I still felt dissatisfied, yet did not utter a word of dissatisfaction. Without accepting his doctrine, without embracing it, I got up from my seat and left.

The Doctrine of Ajita Kesakambala

21. "Another time, venerable sir, I approached Ajita Kesakambala, exchanged greetings and courtesies with him, and sat down to one side. I then asked him (*as in* §14) if he could point out a fruit of recluseship visible here and now.

22. "When I had finished speaking, Ajita Kesakambala said to me: 'Great king, there is no giving, no offering, no liberality. There is no fruit or result of good and bad actions. There is no present world, no world beyond, no mother, no father, no beings who have taken rebirth. In the world there are no recluses and brahmins of right attainment and right practice who explain this world and the world beyond on the basis of their own direct knowledge and realization. A person is composed of the four primary elements. When he dies, the earth (in his body) returns to and merges with the (external) body of earth; the water (in his body) returns to and merges with the (external) body of water; the fire (in his body) returns to and merges with the (external) body of fire; the air (in his body) returns to and merges with the (external) body of air. His sense faculties pass over into space. Four men carry the corpse along on a bier. His eulogies are sounded until they reach the charnel ground. His bones turn pigeon-colored. His meritorious offerings end in ashes. The practice of giving is a doctrine of fools. Those who declare that there is (an afterlife) speak only false, empty prattle. With the breaking up of the body, the foolish and the wise alike are annihilated and utterly perish. They do not exist after death.'

23. "Thus, venerable sir, when I asked Ajita Kesakambala about a visible fruit of recluseship, he explained to me (his doctrine of) annihilation. Venerable sir, just as if one asked about a mango would speak about a breadfruit, or as if one asked about a breadfruit would speak about a mango, in the same way, when I asked Ajita Kesakambala about a visible fruit of recluseship, he explained to me (his doctrine of) annihilation. Then, venerable sir, I thought to myself: 'One like myself should not think of troubling a recluse or brahmin living in his realm.' So I neither rejoiced in the statement of Ajita Kesakambala nor did I reject it. But though I neither rejoiced in it nor rejected it, I still felt dissatisfied, yet did not utter a word of dissatisfaction. Without accepting his doctrine, without embracing it, I got up from my seat and left.

The Doctrine of Pakudha Kaccāyana

24. "Another time, venerable sir, I approached Pakudha Kaccāyana, exchanged greetings and courtesies with him, and sat down to one side. I then asked him (*as in* §14) if he could point out a fruit of recluseship visible here and now.

25. "When I had finished speaking, Pakudha Kaccāyana said to me: 'Great king, there are seven bodies that are unmade, unfashioned, uncreated, without a creator, barren, stable as a mountain peak, standing firm like a pillar. They do not alter, do not change, do not obstruct one another; they are incapable of causing one another either pleasure or pain, or both pleasure and pain. What are the seven? The body of earth, the body of water, the body of fire, the body of air, pleasure, pain, and the soul as the seventh. Among these there is no killer nor one who causes killing; no hearer nor one who causes hearing; no cognizer nor one who causes cognition. If someone were to cut off (another person's) head with a sharp sword, he would not be taking (the other's) life. The sword merely passes through the space between the seven bodies.'

26. "Thus, venerable sir, when I asked Pakudha Kaccāyana about a visible fruit of recluseship, he answered me in a

completely irrelevant way. Venerable sir, just as if one asked about a mango would speak about a breadfruit, or as if one asked about a breadfruit would speak about a mango, in the same way, when I asked Pakudha Kaccāyana about a visible fruit of recluseship, he answered me in a completely irrelevant way. Then, venerable sir, I thought to myself: 'One like myself should not think of troubling a recluse or brahmin living in his realm.' So I neither rejoiced in the statement of Pakudha Kaccāyana nor did I reject it. But though I neither rejoiced in it nor rejected it, I still felt dissatisfied, yet did not utter a word of dissatisfaction. Without accepting his doctrine, without embracing it, I got up from my seat and left.

The Doctrine of Nigaṇṭha Nātaputta

27. "Another time, venerable sir, I approached Nigaṇṭha Nātaputta, exchanged greetings and courtesies with him, and sat down to one side. I then asked him (*as in* §14) if he could point out a fruit of recluseship visible here and now.

28. "When I had finished speaking, Nigaṇṭha Nātaputta said to me: 'Great king, a Nigaṇṭha, a knotless one, is restrained with a fourfold restraint. How so? Herein, great king, a Nigaṇṭha is restrained with regard to all water; he is endowed with the avoidance of all evil; he is cleansed by the avoidance of all evil; he is suffused with the avoidance of all evil. Great king, when a Nigaṇṭha is restrained with this fourfold restraint, he is called a knotless one who is self-perfected, self-controlled, and self-established.'

29. "Thus, venerable sir, when I asked Nigaṇṭha Nātaputta about a visible fruit of recluseship, he explained to me the fourfold restraint. Venerable sir, just as if one asked about a mango would speak about a breadfruit, or as if one asked about a breadfruit would speak about a mango, in the same way, when I asked Nigaṇṭha Nātaputta about a visible fruit of recluseship, he explained to me the fourfold restraint. Then, venerable sir, I thought to myself: 'One like myself should not think of troubling a recluse or brahmin living in his realm.' So I neither rejoiced

in the statement of Nigaṇṭha Nātaputta, nor did I reject it. But though I neither rejoiced in it nor rejected it, I still felt dissatisfied, yet did not utter a word of dissatisfaction. Without accepting his doctrine, without embracing it, I got up from my seat and left.

The Doctrine of Sañjaya Belaṭṭhaputta

30. "Another time, venerable sir, I approached Sañjaya Belaṭṭhaputta, exchanged greetings and courtesies with him, and sat down to one side. I then asked him (*as in* §14) if he could point out any fruit of recluseship visible here and now.

31. "When I had finished speaking, Sañjaya Belaṭṭhaputta said to me: 'If you ask me:

A. 1. "Is there a world beyond?" If I thought that there is a world beyond, I would declare to you "There is a world beyond." But I do not say "It is this way," nor "It is that way," nor "It is otherwise." I do not say "It is not so," nor do I say "It is not not so."

'Similarly, you might ask me the following questions:

A. 2. "Is there no world beyond?"
3. "Is it that there both is and is not a world beyond?"
4. "Is it that there neither is nor is not a world beyond?"

B. 1. "Are there beings who have taken rebirth?"
2. "Are there no beings who have taken rebirth?"
3. "Is it that there both are and are not beings who have taken rebirth?"
4. "Is it that there neither are nor are not beings who have taken rebirth?"

C. 1. "Is there fruit and result of good and bad actions?"
2. "Is there no fruit and result of good and bad actions?"
3. "Is it that there both are and are not fruit and result of good and bad actions?"
4. "Is it that there neither are nor are not fruit and result of good and bad actions?"

D. 1. "Does the *Tathāgata* exist after death?"
2. "Does the *Tathāgata* not exist after death?"
3. "Does the *Tathāgata* both exist and not exist after death?"
4. "Does the *Tathāgata* neither exist nor not exist after death?"

'If I thought that it was so, I would declare to you "It is so." But do I not say "It is this way," nor "It is that way," nor "It is otherwise." I do not say "It is not so," nor do I say "It is not not so."'

32. "Thus, venerable sir, when I asked Sañjaya Belaṭṭhaputta about a visible fruit of recluseship, he answered me evasively. Venerable sir, just as if one asked about a mango would speak about a breadfruit, or as if one asked about a breadfruit would speak about a mango, in the same way, when I asked Sañjaya Belaṭṭhaputta about a visible fruit of recluseship, he answered me evasively. Then, venerable sir, I thought to myself: 'One like myself should not think of troubling a recluse or brahmin living in his realm.' So I neither rejoiced in the statement of Sañjaya Belaṭṭhaputta nor did I reject it. But though I neither rejoiced in it nor rejected it, I still felt dissatisfied, yet did not utter a word of dissatisfaction. Without accepting his doctrine, without embracing it, I got up from my seat and left.

The First Visible Fruit of Recluseship

33. "So, venerable sir, I ask the Exalted One: There are, venerable sir, various crafts, such as elephant trainers, horse trainers, charioteers, archers, standard bearers, camp marshals, commandos, high royal officers, front-line soldiers, bull-warriors, military heroes, mail-clad warriors, domestic slaves, confectioners, barbers, bath attendants, cooks, garland-makers, laundrymen, weavers, basketmakers, potters, statisticians, accountants, and various other crafts of a similar nature. All those (who practise these crafts) enjoy here and now the visible fruits of their craft. They obtain happiness and joy themselves, and they give happiness and joy to their

parents, their wives and children, their friends and colleagues. They establish an excellent presentation of gifts to recluses and brahmins—leading to heaven, ripening in happiness, conducing to a heavenly rebirth. Is it possible, venerable sir, to point out any fruit of recluseship that is similarly visible here and now?"

34. "It is, great king. But let me question you about this matter. Answer as you think fit.

"What do you think, great king? Suppose you have a slave, a workman who rises up before you, retires after you, does whatever you want, acts always for your pleasure, speaks politely to you, and is ever on the lookout to see that you are satisfied. The thought might occur to him: 'It is wonderful and marvellous, the destiny and result of meritorious deeds. For this King Ajātasattu is a human being, and I too am a human being, yet King Ajātasattu enjoys himself fully endowed and supplied with the five strands of sense pleasure as if he were a god, while I am his slave, his workman—rising before him, retiring after him, doing whatever he wants, acting always for his pleasure, speaking politely to him, ever on the lookout to see that he is satisfied. I could be like him if I were to do meritorious deeds. Let me then shave off my hair and beard, put on saffron robes, and go forth from home to homelessness.'

"After some time he shaves off his hair and beard, puts on saffron robes, and goes forth from home to homelessness. Having gone forth he dwells restrained in body, speech, and mind, content with the simplest food and shelter, delighting in solitude. Suppose your men were to report all this to you. Would you say: 'Bring that man back to me, men. Let him again become my slave, my workman, rising before me, retiring after me, doing whatever I want, acting always for my pleasure, speaking politely to me, ever on the lookout to see that I am satisfied.'?"

35. "Certainly not, venerable sir. Rather, we would pay homage to him, rise up out of respect for him, invite him to a seat, and invite him to accept from us robes, almsfood, dwelling and medicinal requirements. And we would provide him righteous protection, defense, and security."

36. "What do you think, great king? If such is the case, is there or is there not a visible fruit of recluseship?"

"There certainly is, venerable sir."

"This, great king, is the first fruit of recluseship, visible here and now, that I point out to you."

The Second Visible Fruit of Recluseship

37. "Is it possible, venerable sir, to point out some other fruit of recluseship visible here and now?"

"It is, great king. But let me question you about this matter. Answer as you think fit.

"What do you think, great king? Suppose there is a farmer, a householder, who pays taxes to maintain the royal revenue. The thought might occur to him: 'It is wonderful and marvellous, the destiny and result of meritorious deeds. For this King Ajātasattu is a human being, and I too am a human being. Yet King Ajātasattu enjoys himself fully endowed and supplied with the five strands of sense pleasure as if he were a god, while I am a farmer, a householder, who pays taxes to maintain the royal revenue. I could be like him if I were to do meritorious deeds. Let me then shave off my hair and beard, put on saffron robes, and go forth from home to homelessness.'

"After some time, he abandons his accumulation of wealth, be it large or small, abandons his circle of relatives, be it large or small; he shaves off his hair and beard, puts on saffron robes, and goes forth from home to homelessness. Having gone forth, he dwells restrained in body, speech, and mind, content with the simplest food and shelter, delighting in solitude. Suppose your men were to report all this to you. Would you say: 'Bring that man back to me, men. Let him again become a farmer, a householder, who pays taxes to maintain the royal revenue'?"

38. "Certainly not, venerable sir. Rather, we would pay homage to him, rise up out of respect for him, invite him to a seat, and invite him to accept from us robes, almsfood, dwelling, and medicinal requirements. And we would provide him with righteous protection, defense, and security."

39. "What do you think, great king? If such is the case, is there or is there not a visible fruit of recluseship?"

"There certainly is, venerable sir."

"This, great king, is the second fruit of recluseship, visible here and now, that I point out to you."

The More Excellent Fruits of Recluseship

40. "Is it possible, venerable sir, to point out any other fruit of recluseship visible here and now, more excellent and sublime than these two fruits?"

"It is possible. Listen, great king, and attend carefully, I will speak."

"Yes, venerable sir," King Ajātasattu replied to the Exalted One.

41. The Exalted One spoke: "Herein, great king, a *Tathāgata* arises in the world, a worthy one, perfectly enlightened, endowed with clear knowledge and conduct, accomplished, a knower of the world, unsurpassed trainer of men to be tamed, teacher of gods and men, enlightened and exalted. Having realized by his own direct knowledge this world with its gods, its Māras, and its Brahmās, this generation with its recluses and brahmins, its rulers and people, he makes it known to others. He teaches the *Dhamma* that is good in the beginning, good in the middle, and good in the end, possessing meaning and phrasing; he reveals the holy life that is fully complete and purified.[8]

42. "A householder, or a householder's son, or one born into some other family, hears the *Dhamma*. Having heard the *Dhamma*, he gains faith in the *Tathāgata*. Endowed with such faith, he reflects: 'The household life is crowded, a path of dust. Going forth is like the open air. It is not easy for one dwelling at home to lead the perfectly complete, perfectly

---

8. In this translation the phrase "fully complete and purified" is construed as standing in apposition to "holy life," whereas the commentary (see below) takes it to stand in apposition to "*Dhamma*." The former inter- pretation seems to be borne out by Section 42.

purified holy life, bright as a polished conch. Let me then shave off my hair and beard, put on saffron robes, and go forth from home to homelessness.'

43. "After some time he abandons his accumulation of wealth, be it large or small; he abandons his circle of relatives, be it large or small; he shaves off his hair and beard, puts on saffron robes, and goes forth from home to homelessness.

44. "When he has thus gone forth, he lives restrained by the restraint of the *Pātimokkha*,[9] possessed of proper behavior and resort. Having taken up the rules of training, he trains himself in them, seeing danger in the slightest faults. He comes to be endowed with wholesome bodily and verbal action, his livelihood is purified, and he is possessed of moral discipline. He guards the doors of his sense faculties, is endowed with mindfulness and clear comprehension, and is content.

The Small Section on Moral Discipline

45. "And how, great king, is the *bhikkhu* possessed of moral discipline? Herein, great king, having abandoned the destruction of life, the *bhikkhu* abstains from the destruction of life. He has laid down the rod and weapon and dwells conscientious, full of kindness, sympathetic for the welfare of all living beings. This pertains to his moral discipline.

"Having abandoned taking what is not given, he abstains from taking what is not given. Accepting and expecting only what is given, he lives in honesty with a pure mind. This too pertains to his moral discipline.

"Having abandoned incelibacy, he leads the holy life of celibacy. He dwells aloof and abstains from the vulgar practice of sexual intercourse. This too pertains to his moral discipline.

"Having abandoned false speech, he abstains from falsehood. He speaks only the truth, he lives devoted to truth; trustworthy and reliable, he does not deceive anyone in the world. This too pertains to his moral discipline.

---

9. The code of fundamental monastic rules, 227 in its Pali version.

"Having abandoned slander, he abstains from slander. He does not repeat elsewhere what he has heard here in order to divide others from the people here, nor does he repeat here what he has heard elsewhere in order to divide these from the people there. Thus he is a reconciler of those who are divided and a promoter of friendships. Rejoicing, delighting, and exulting in concord, he speaks only words that are conducive to concord. This too pertains to his moral discipline.

"Having abandoned harsh speech, he abstains from harsh speech. He speaks only such words as are gentle, pleasing to the ear, endearing, going to the heart, polite, amiable and agreeable to the manyfolk. This too pertains to his moral discipline.

"Having abandoned idle chatter, he abstains from idle chatter. He speaks at the right time, speaks what is factual and beneficial, speaks on the *Dhamma* and the Discipline. His words are worth treasuring; they are timely, backed by reasons, measured, and connected with the good. This too pertains to his moral discipline.

"He abstains from damaging seed and plant life.

"He eats only in one part of the day, refraining from food at night and from eating at improper times.

"He abstains from dancing, singing, instrumental music, and from witnessing unsuitable shows.

"He abstains from wearing garlands, embellishing himself with scents, and beautifying himself with unguents.

"He abstains from high and luxurious beds and seats.

"He abstains from accepting gold and silver.

"He abstains from accepting uncooked grain, raw meat, women and girls, male and female slaves, goats and sheep, fowl and swine, elephants, cattle, horses and mares.

"He abstains from accepting fields and lands.

"He abstains from running messages and errands.

"He abstains from buying and selling.

"He abstains from dealing with false weights, false metals, and false measures.

"He abstains from the crooked ways of bribery, deception, and fraud.

"He abstains from mutilating, executing, imprisoning, robbery, plunder, and violence.

"This too pertains to his moral discipline.

The Intermediate Section on Moral Discipline

46. "Whereas some recluses and brahmins, while living on food offered by the faithful, continually cause damage to seed and plant life—to plants propagated from roots, stems, joints, buddings, and seeds—he abstains from damaging seed and plant life. This too pertains to his moral discipline.

47. "Whereas some recluses and brahmins, while living on food offered by the faithful, enjoy the use of stored-up goods, such as stored-up food, drinks, garments, vehicles, bedding, scents, and comestibles—he abstains from the use of stored-up goods. This too pertains to his moral discipline.

48. "Whereas some recluses and brahmins, while living on food offered by the faithful, attend unsuitable shows, such as:

shows featuring dancing, singing, or instrumental music;
theatrical performances;
narrations of legends;
music played by hand-clapping, cymbals, and drums;
picture houses;
acrobatic performances;
combats of elephants, horses, buffaloes, bulls, goats, rams, cocks and quails;
stick-fights, boxing, and wrestling;
sham-fights, roll-calls, battle-arrays, and regimental reviews—

he abstains from attending such unsuitable shows. This too pertains to his moral discipline.

49. "Whereas some recluses and brahmins, while living on food offered by the faithful, indulge in the following games and recreations[10]:

---

10. The explanations of these games are drawn from the commentary.

aṭṭhapada (a game played on an eight-row chessboard);
dasapada (a game played on a ten-row chessboard);
ākāsa (played by imagining a board in the air);
parihārapatha ("hopscotch," a diagram is drawn on the ground and one has to jump in the allowable spaces avoiding the lines);
santika ("spillikins," assembling the pieces in a pile, removing and returning them without disturbing the pile);
khalika (dice games);
ghaṭika (hitting a short stick with a long stick);
salākahattha (a game played by dipping the hand in paint or dye, striking the ground or a wall, and requiring the participants to show the figure of an elephant, a horse etc.);
akkha (ball games);
paṅgacīra (blowing through toy pipes made of leaves);
vaṅkaka (ploughing with miniature ploughs);
mokkhacika (turning somersaults);
ciṅgulika (playing with paper windmills);
pattāḷaka (playing with toy measures);
rathaka (playing with toy chariots);
dhanuka (playing with toy bows);
akkharika (guessing at letters written in the air or on one's back);
manesika (guessing others' thoughts);
yathāvajja (games involving mimicry of deformities)—

he abstains from such games that are a basis for negligence. This too pertains to his moral discipline.

50. "Whereas some recluses and brahmins, while living on food offered by the faithful, enjoy the use of high and luxurious beds and seats, such as:

spacious couches;
thrones with animal figures carved on the supports;
long-haired coverlets;
multi-colored patchwork coverlets;
white woollen coverlets;
woollen coverlets embroidered with flowers;
quilts stuffed with cotton;

woollen coverlets embroidered with animal figures;
woollen coverlets with hair on both sides or on one side;
bedspreads embroidered with gems;
silk coverlets;
dance-hall carpets;
elephant, horse, or chariot rugs;
rugs of antelope-skins;
choice spreads made of *kadali*-deer hides;
spreads with red awnings overhead;
couches with red cushions for head and feet—

he abstains from the use of such high and luxurious beds and seats. This too pertains to his moral discipline.

51. "Whereas some recluses and brahmins, while living on food offered by the faithful, enjoy the use of such devices for embellishing and beautifying themselves as the following: rubbing scented powders into the body, massaging with oils, bathing in perfumed water, kneading the limbs, mirrors, ointments, garlands, scents, unguents, face-powders, make-up, bracelets, head-bands, decorated walking sticks, ornamented medicine-tubes, rapiers, sunshades, embroidered sandals, turbans, diadems, yaktail whisks, and long-fringed white robes—he abstains from the use of such devices for embellishment and beautification. This too pertains to his moral discipline.

52. "Whereas some recluses and brahmins, while living on the food offered by the faithful, engage in frivolous chatter, such as: talk about kings, thieves, and ministers of state; talk about armies, dangers, and wars; talk about food, drink, garments, and lodgings; talk about garlands and scents; talk about relations, vehicles, villages, towns, cities, and countries; talk about women and talk about heroes; street talk and talk by the well; talk about those departed in days gone by; rambling chit-chat; speculations about the world and about the sea; talk about gain and loss—he abstains from such frivolous chatter. This too pertains to his moral discipline.

53. "Whereas some recluses and brahmins, while living on the food offered by the faithful, engage in wrangling argumentation (saying to one another):

'You don't understand this doctrine and discipline. It is I who understand this doctrine and discipline.'
'How can you understand this doctrine and discipline?'
'You're practising the wrong way. I'm practicing the right way.'
'I'm being consistent. You're inconsistent.'
'What should have been said first you said last, what should have been said last you said first.'
'What you took so long to think out has been confuted.'
'Your doctrine has been refuted. You're defeated. Go, try to save your doctrine, or disentangle yourself now if you can'—

he abstains from such wrangling argumentation. This too pertains to his moral discipline.

54. "Whereas some recluses and brahmins, while living on the food offered by the faithful, engage in running messages and errands for kings, ministers of state, *khattiyas*, brahmins, householders, or youths, (who command them): 'Go here, go there, take this, bring that from there'—he abstains from running such messages and errands. This too pertains to his moral discipline.

55. "Whereas some recluses and brahmins, while living on the food offered by the faithful, engage in scheming, talking, hinting, belittling others, and pursuing gain with gain, he abstains from such kinds of scheming and talking.[11] This too pertains to his moral discipline.

11. Improper ways of gaining material support from donors, discussed in detail in Vism 1.61–82, pp. 24–30.

The Large Section on Moral Discipline

56. "Whereas some recluses and brahmins, while living on the food offered by the faithful, earn their living by a wrong means of livelihood, by such debased arts as:[12]

prophesying long life, prosperity etc., or the reverse, from the marks on a person's limbs, hands, feet, etc;
divining by means of omens and signs;
making auguries on the basis of thunderbolts and celestial portents;
interpreting ominous dreams;
telling fortunes from marks on the body;
making auguries from the marks on cloth gnawed by mice;
offering fire oblations;
offering oblations from a ladle;
offering oblations of husks, rice powder, rice grains, ghee and oil to the gods;
offering oblations from the mouth;
offering blood-sacrifices to the gods;
making predictions based on the fingertips;
determining whether the site for a proposed house or garden is propitious or not;
making predictions for officers of state;
laying demons in a cemetery;
laying ghosts;
knowledge of charms to be pronounced by one living in an earthen house;
snake charming;
the poison craft, scorpion craft, rat craft, bird craft, crow craft;
foretelling the number of years that a man has to live;
reciting charms to give protection from arrows;
reciting charms to understand the language of animals—

he abstains from such wrong means of livelihood, from such debased arts. This too pertains to his moral discipline.

---

12. The explanation of these arts, usually indicated by a single obscure word in the text, is drawn from the commentary.

57. "Whereas some recluses and brahmins, while living on the food offered by the faithful, earn their living by a wrong means of livelihood, by such debased arts as interpreting the significance of the color, shape, and other features of the following items to determine whether they portend fortune or misfortune for their owners: gems, garments, staffs, swords, spears, arrows, bows, other weapons, women, men, boys, girls, slaves, slave-women, elephants, horses, buffaloes, bulls, cows, goats, rams, fowl, quails, lizards, earrings (or house-gables), tortoises, and other animals—

he abstains from such wrong means of livelihood, from such debased arts. This too pertains to his moral discipline.

58. "Whereas some recluses and brahmins, while living on the food offered by the faithful, earn their living by a wrong means of livelihood, by such debased arts as making predictions to the effect that:

> the king will march forth;
> the king will return;
> our king will attack and the enemy king will retreat;
> our enemy king will attack and our king will retreat;
> our king will triumph and the enemy king will be defeated;
> the enemy king will triumph and our king will be defeated;
> thus there will be victory for one and defeat for the other—

he abstains from such wrong means of livelihood, from such debased arts. This too pertains to his moral discipline.

59. "Whereas some recluses and brahmins, while living on the food offered by the faithful, earn their living by a wrong means of livelihood, by such debased arts as predicting: there will be an eclipse of the moon, an eclipse of the sun, an eclipse of a constellation; the sun and the moon will go on their proper courses; there will be an aberration of the sun and moon; the constellations will go on their proper courses; there will be an aberration of a constellation; there will be a fall of meteors; there will be a skyblaze; there will be an earthquake; there will be an earth-roar; there will be a rising and setting, a darkening and brightening of the moon, sun, and constellations; such

will be the result of the moon's eclipse, such the result of the sun's eclipse, (and so on down to) such will be the result of the rising and setting, darkening and brightening of the moon, sun, and constellations—he abstains from such wrong means of livelihood, from such debased arts. This too pertains to his moral discipline.

60. "Whereas some recluses and brahmins, while living on the food offered by the faithful, earn their living by a wrong means of livelihood, by such debased arts as predicting: there will be abundant rain; there will be a drought; there will be a good harvest; there will be a famine; there will be security; there will be danger; there will be sickness; there will be health; or they earn their living by accounting, computation, calculation, the composing of poetry, and speculations about the world—he abstains from such wrong means of livelihood, from such debased arts. This too pertains to his moral discipline.

61. "Whereas some recluses and brahmins, while living on the food offered by the faithful, earn their living by a wrong means of livelihood, by such debased arts as: arranging auspicious dates for marriages, both those in which the bride is brought home and those in which she is sent out; arranging auspicious dates for betrothals and divorces; arranging auspicious dates for the accumulation or expenditure of money; reciting charms to make people lucky or unlucky; rejuvenating the fetuses of abortive women; reciting spells to bind a man's tongue, to paralyze his jaws, to make him lose control over his hands, or to bring on deafness; obtaining oracular answers to questions by means of a mirror, a girl, or a god; worshipping the sun; worshipping Mahābrahmā; bringing forth flames from the mouth; invoking the goddess of luck—he abstains from such wrong means of livelihood, from such debased arts. This too pertains to his moral discipline.

62. "Whereas some recluses and brahmins, while living on the food offered by the faithful, earn their living by a wrong means of livelihood, by such debased arts as: promising gifts to deities in return for favours; fulfilling such promises; demonology; reciting spells after entering an earthen house; inducing virility

and impotence; preparing and consecrating sites for a house; giving ceremonial mouthwashes and ceremonial bathing; offering sacrificial fires; administering emetics, purgatives, expectorants, and phlegmagogues; administering medicines through the ear and through the nose, administering ointments and counter-ointments, practising fine surgery on the eyes and ears, practising general surgery on the body, practising as a children's doctor—he abstains from such wrong means of livelihood, from such debased arts. This too pertains to his moral discipline.

63. "Great king, the *bhikkhu* who is thus possessed of moral discipline sees no danger anywhere in regard to his restraint by moral discipline. Just as a head-anointed noble warrior who has defeated his enemies sees no danger anywhere from his enemies, so the *bhikkhu* who is thus possessed of moral discipline sees no danger anywhere in regard to his restraint by moral discipline. Endowed with this noble aggregate of moral discipline, he experiences within himself a blameless happiness. In this way, great king, the *bhikkhu* is possessed of moral discipline.

Restraint of the Sense Faculties

64. "And how, great king, does the *bhikkhu* guard the doors of his sense faculties? Herein, great king, having seen a form with the eye, the *bhikkhu* does not grasp at the sign or the details. Since, if he were to dwell without restraint over the faculty of the eye, evil unwholesome states such as covetousness and grief might assail him, he practises restraint, guards the faculty of the eye, and achieves restraint over the faculty of the eye. Having heard a sound with the ear … having smelled an odour with the nose … having tasted a flavour with the tongue … having touched a tangible object with the body … having cognized a mind-object with the mind, the *bhikkhu* does not grasp at the sign or the details. Since, if he were to dwell without restraint over the faculty of the mind, evil unwholesome states such as covetousness and grief might assail him, he practises restraint, guards the faculty of the mind, and achieves restraint over the faculty of the mind.

Endowed with this noble restraint of the sense faculties, he experiences within himself an unblemished happiness. In this way, great king, the *bhikkhu* guards the doors of the sense faculties.

Mindfulness and Clear Comprehension

65. "And how, great king, is the *bhikkhu* endowed with mindfulness and clear comprehension? Herein, great king, in going forward and returning, the *bhikkhu* acts with clear comprehension. In looking ahead and looking aside, he acts with clear comprehension. In bending and stretching the limbs, he acts with clear comprehension. In wearing his robes and cloak and using his almsbowl, he acts with clear comprehension. In eating, drinking, chewing, and tasting, he acts with clear comprehension. In defecating and urinating, he acts with clear comprehension. In going, standing, sitting, lying down, waking up, speaking, and remaining silent, he acts with clear comprehension. In this way, great king, the *bhikkhu* is endowed with mindfulness and clear comprehension.

Contentment

66. "And how, great king, is the *bhikkhu* content? Herein, great king, a *bhikkhu* is content with robes to protect his body and almsfood to sustain his belly; wherever he goes he sets out taking only (his requisites) along with him. Just as a bird, wherever it goes, flies with its wings as its only burden, in the same way a *bhikkhu* is content with robes to protect his body and almsfood to sustain his belly; wherever he goes he sets out taking only (his requisites) along with him. In this way, great king, the *bhikkhu* is content.

The Abandoning of the Hindrances

67. "Endowed with this noble aggregate of moral discipline, this noble restraint over the sense faculties, this noble mindfulness and clear comprehension, and this noble

contentment, he resorts to a secluded dwelling—a forest, the foot of a tree, a mountain, a glen, a hillside cave, a cremation ground, a jungle grove, the open air, a heap of straw. After returning from his almsround, following his meals, he sits down, crosses his legs, holds his body erect, and sets up mindfulness before him.

68. "Having abandoned covetousness for the world, he dwells with a mind free from covetousness; he purifies his mind from covetousness. Having abandoned ill will and hatred, he dwells with a benevolent mind, sympathetic for the welfare of all living beings; he purifies his mind from ill will and hatred. Having abandoned dullness and drowsiness, he dwells perceiving light, mindful and clearly comprehending; he purifies his mind from dullness and drowsiness. Having abandoned restlessness and worry, he dwells at ease within himself, with a peaceful mind; he purifies his mind from restlessness and worry. Having abandoned doubt, he dwells as one who has passed beyond doubt, unperplexed about wholesome states; he purifies his mind from doubt.

69. "Great king, suppose a man were to take a loan and apply it to his business, and his business were to succeed, so that he could pay back his old debts and would have enough money left over to maintain a wife. He would reflect on this, and as a result he would become glad and experience joy.

70. "Again, great king, suppose a man were to become sick, afflicted, gravely ill, so that he could not enjoy his food and his strength would decline. After some time he would recover from that illness and would enjoy his food and regain his bodily strength. He would reflect on this, and as a result he would become glad and experience joy.

71. "Again, great king, suppose a man were locked up in a prison. After some time he would be released from prison, safe and secure, with no loss of his possessions. He would reflect on this, and as a result he would become glad and experience joy.

72. "Again, great king, suppose a man were a slave, without independence, subservient to others, unable to go where he wants. After some time he would be released from slavery and gain his independence; he would no longer be subservient to others but a

free man able to go where he wants. He would reflect on this, and as a result he would become glad and experience joy.

73. "Again, great king, suppose a man with wealth and possessions were travelling along a desert road where food was scarce and dangers were many. After some time he would cross over the desert and arrive safely at a village which is safe and free from danger. He would reflect on this, and as a result he would become glad and experience joy.

74. "In the same way, great king, when a *bhikkhu* sees that these five hindrances are unabandoned within himself, he regards that as a debt, as a sickness, as confinement in prison, as slavery, as a desert road.

75. "But when he sees that these five hindrances have been abandoned within himself, he regards that as freedom from debt, as good health, as release from prison, as freedom from slavery, as a place of safety.

76. "When he sees that these five hindrances have been abandoned within himself, gladness arises. When he is gladdened, rapture arises. When his mind is filled with rapture, his body becomes tranquil; tranquil in body, he experiences happiness; being happy, his mind becomes concentrated.

The First *Jhāna*

77. "Quite secluded from sense pleasures, secluded from unwholesome states, he enters and dwells in the first *Jhāna*, which is accompanied by applied and sustained thought and filled with the rapture and happiness born of seclusion. He drenches, steeps, saturates, and suffuses his body with this rapture and happiness born of seclusion, so that there is no part of his entire body which is not suffused by this rapture and happiness.

78. "Great king, suppose a skilled bath attendant or his apprentice were to pour soap-powder into a metal basin, sprinkle it with water, and knead it into a ball, so that the ball of soap-powder be pervaded by moisture, encompassed by moisture, suffused with moisture inside and out, yet would not trickle. In the same way, great king, the *bhikkhu* drenches, steeps, saturates,

and suffuses his body with the rapture and happiness born of seclusion, so that there is no part of his entire body which is not suffused by this rapture and happiness. This, great king, is a visible fruit of recluseship more excellent and sublime than the previous ones.

The Second *Jhāna*

79. "Further, great king, with the subsiding of applied and sustained thought, the *bhikkhu* enters and dwells in the second *Jhāna*, which is accompanied by internal confidence and unification of mind, is without applied and sustained thought, and is filled with the rapture and happiness born of concentration. He drenches, steeps, saturates, and suffuses his body with this rapture and happiness born of concentration, so that there is no part of his entire body which is not suffused by this rapture and happiness.

80. "Great king, suppose there were a deep lake whose waters welled up from below. It would have no inlet for water from the east, west, north, or south, nor would it be refilled from time to time with showers of rain; yet a current of cool water, welling up from within the lake, would drench, steep, saturate and suffuse the whole lake, so that there would be no part of that entire lake which is not suffused with the cool water. In the same way, great king, the *bhikkhu* drenches, steeps, saturates, and suffuses his body with the rapture and happiness born of concentration, so that there is no part of his entire body which is not suffused by this rapture and happiness. This too, great king, is a visible fruit of recluseship more excellent and sublime than the previous ones.

The Third *Jhāna*

81. "Further, great king, with the fading away of rapture, the *bhikkhu* dwells in equanimity, mindful and clearly comprehending, and experiences happiness with the body. Thus he enters and dwells in the third *Jhāna*, of which the noble ones declare: 'He dwells happily with equanimity and mindfulness.' He drenches, steeps, saturates, and suffuses his body with this

happiness free from rapture, so that there is no part of his entire body which is not suffused by this happiness.

82. "Great king, suppose in a lotus pond there were blue, white, or red lotuses that have been born in the water, grow in the water, and never rise up above the water, but flourish immersed in the water. From their tips to their roots they would be drenched, steeped, saturated, and suffused with cool water, so that there would be no part of those lotuses not suffused with cool water. In the same way, great king, the *bhikkhu* drenches, steeps, saturates and suffuses his body with the happiness free from rapture, so that there is no part of his entire body which is not suffused by this happiness. This too, great king, is a visible fruit of recluseship more excellent and sublime than the previous ones.

The Fourth *Jhāna*

83. "Further, great king, with the abandoning of pleasure and pain, and with the previous passing away of joy and grief, the *bhikkhu* enters and dwells in the fourth *Jhāna*, which is neither pleasant nor painful and contains mindfulness fully purified by equanimity. He sits suffusing his body with a pure bright mind, so that there is no part of his entire body not suffused by a pure bright mind.

84. "Great king, suppose a man were to be sitting covered from the head down by a white cloth, so that there would be no part of his entire body not suffused by the white cloth. In the same way, great king, the *bhikkhu* sits suffusing his body with a pure bright mind, so that there is no part of his entire body not suffused by a pure bright mind. This too, great king, is a visible fruit of recluseship more excellent and sublime than the previous ones.

Insight Knowledge

85. "When his mind is thus concentrated, pure and bright, unblemished, free from defects, malleable, wieldy, steady and attained to imperturbability, he directs and inclines it to knowledge and vision. He understands thus: 'This is my

body, having material form, composed of the four primary elements, originating from father and mother, built up out of rice and gruel, impermanent, subject to rubbing and pressing, to dissolution and dispersion. And this is my consciousness, supported by it and bound up with it.'

86. "Great king, suppose there were a beautiful beryl gem of purest water, eight-faceted, well-cut, clear, limpid, flawless, endowed with all excellent qualities. And through it there would run a blue, yellow, red, white, or brown thread. A man with keen sight, taking it in his hand, would reflect upon it thus: 'This is a beautiful beryl gem of purest water, eight-faceted, well-cut, clear, limpid, flawless, endowed with all excellent qualities. And running through it there is this blue, yellow, red, white, or brown thread.' In the same way, great king, when his mind is thus concentrated, pure and bright … the *bhikkhu* directs and inclines it to knowledge and vision and understands thus: 'This is my body, having material form … . and this is my consciousness, supported by it and bound up with it.' This, too, great king, is a visible fruit of recluseship more excellent and sublime than the previous ones.

The Knowledge of the Mind-made Body

87. "When his mind is thus concentrated, pure and bright, unblemished, free from defects, malleable, wieldy, steady, and attained to imperturbability, he directs and inclines it to creating a mind-made body. From this body he creates another body having material form, mind-made, complete in all its parts, not lacking any faculties.

88. "Great king, suppose a man were to draw out a reed from its sheath. He would think: 'This is the reed; this is the sheath. The reed is one thing, the sheath another, but the reed has been drawn out from the sheath.' Or suppose a man were to draw a sword out from its scabbard. He would think: 'This is the sword; this is the scabbard. The sword is one thing, the scabbard another, but the sword has been drawn out from the scabbard.' Or suppose a man were to pull a snake out from its slough. He would think: 'This

is the snake; this is the slough. The snake is one thing, the slough another, but the snake has been pulled out from the slough.' In the same way, great king, when his mind is thus concentrated, pure and bright … The *bhikkhu* directs and inclines it to creating a mind-made body. From this body he creates another body having material form, mind-made, complete in all its parts, not lacking any faculties. This too, great king, is a visible fruit of recluseship more excellent and sublime than the previous ones.

The Knowledge of the Modes of Supernormal Power

89. "When his mind is thus concentrated, pure and bright, unblemished, free from defects, malleable, wieldy, steady, and attained to imperturbability, he directs and inclines it to the modes of supernormal power. He exercises the various modes of supernormal power: having been one, he becomes many and having been many, he becomes one; he appears and vanishes; he goes unimpeded through walls, ramparts, and mountains as if through space; he dives in and out of the earth as if it were water; he walks on water without sinking as if it were earth; sitting crosslegged he travels through space like a winged bird; with his hand he touches and strokes the sun and the moon, so mighty and powerful; he exercises mastery over the body as far as the Brahma-world.

90. "Great king, suppose a skilled potter or his apprentice were to make and fashion out of well-prepared clay whatever kind of vessel he might desire. Or suppose a skilled ivory-worker or his apprentice were to make and fashion out of well-prepared ivory whatever kind of ivory work he might desire. Or suppose a skilled goldsmith or his apprentice were to make and fashion out of well-prepared gold whatever kind of gold work he might desire. In the same way, great king, when his mind is thus concentrated, pure and bright … the *bhikkhu* directs and inclines it to the modes of supernormal power and exercises the various modes of supernormal power. This too, great king, is a visible fruit of recluseship more excellent and sublime than the previous ones.

The Knowledge of the Divine Ear

91. "When his mind is thus concentrated, pure and bright, unblemished, free from defects, malleable, wieldy, steady, and attained to imperturbability, he directs and inclines it to the divine ear-element. With the divine ear-element, which is purified and surpasses the human, he hears both kinds of sound, the divine and the human, those which are distant and those which are near.

92. "Great king, suppose a man travelling along a highway were to hear the sounds of kettledrums, tabours, horns, cymbals and tomtoms, and would think: 'This is the sound of kettledrums, this is the sound of tabours, this the sound of horns, cymbals and tomtoms.' In the same way, great king, when his mind is thus concentrated, pure and bright … the *bhikkhu* directs and inclines it to the divine ear-element. With the divine ear-element, which is purified and surpasses the human, he hears both kinds of sound, the divine and the human, those which are distant and those which are near. This too, great king, is a visible fruit of recluseship more excellent and sublime than the previous ones.

The Knowledge Encompassing the Minds of Others

93. "When his mind is thus concentrated, pure and bright, unblemished, free from defects, malleable, wieldy, steady, and attained to imperturbability, he directs and inclines it to the knowledge of encompassing the minds (of others). He understands the minds of other beings and persons, having encompassed them with his own mind. He understands a mind with lust as a mind with lust and a mind without lust as a mind without lust; he understands a mind with hatred as a mind with hatred and a mind without hatred as a mind without hatred; he understands a mind with delusion as a mind with delusion and a mind without delusion as a mind without delusion; he understands a contracted mind as a contracted mind and a distracted mind as a distracted mind; he understands an exalted mind as an exalted mind and an unexalted mind as an unexalted

mind; he understands a surpassable mind as a surpassable mind and an unsurpassable mind as an unsurpassable mind; he understands a concentrated mind as a concentrated mind and an unconcentrated mind as an unconcentrated mind; he understands a liberated mind as a liberated mind and an unliberated mind as an unliberated mind.

94. "Great king, suppose a young man or woman, fond of ornaments, examining his or her own facial reflection in a pure bright mirror or in a bowl of clear water, would know, if there were a mole, 'It has a mole,' and if there were no mole, 'It has no mole.' In the same way, great king, when his mind is thus concentrated, pure and bright … the *bhikkhu* directs and inclines it to the knowledge of encompassing the minds (of others). He understands the minds of other beings and persons, having encompassed them with his own mind. This too, great king, is a visible fruit of recluseship more excellent and sublime than the previous ones.

The Knowledge of Recollecting Past Lives

95. "When his mind is thus concentrated, pure and bright, unblemished, free from defects, malleable, wieldy, steady, and attained to imperturbability, he directs and inclines it to the knowledge of recollecting past lives. He recollects his numerous past lives, that is, one birth, two births, three, four, or five births; ten, twenty, thirty, forty, or fifty births; a hundred births, a thousand births, a hundred thousand births; many aeons of world contraction, many aeons of world expansion, many aeons of world contraction and expansion, (recollecting): 'There I had such a name, belonged to such a clan, had such an appearance; such was my food, such my experience of pleasure and pain, such my span of life. Passing away from that state, I re-arose there. There too I had such a name, belonged to such a clan, had such an appearance; such was my food, such my experience of pleasure and pain, such my span of life. Passing away from that state I re-arose here.' Thus he recollects his numerous past lives in their modes and their details.

96. "Great king, suppose a man were to go from his own village to another village, then from that village to still another village, and then from that village he would return to his own village. He would think to himself: 'I went from my own village to that village. There I stood in such a way, sat in such a way, spoke in such a way, and remained silent in such a way. From that village I went to still another village. There too I stood in such a way, sat in such a way, spoke in such a way, and remained silent in such a way. From that village I returned to my own village.' In the same way, great king, when his mind is thus concentrated, pure and bright … the *bhikkhu* directs and inclines it to the knowledge of recollecting past lives, and he recollects his numerous past lives in their modes and their details. This too, great king, is a visible fruit of recluseship, more excellent and sublime than the previous ones.

The Knowledge of the Divine Eye

97. "When his mind is thus concentrated, pure and bright, unblemished, free from defects, malleable, wieldy, steady, and attained to imperturbability, he directs and inclines it to the knowledge of the passing away and reappearance of beings. With the divine eye, which is purified and surpasses the human, he sees beings passing away and reappearing—inferior and superior, beautiful and ugly, fortunate and unfortunate—and he understands how beings fare according to their *kamma*, thus: 'These beings—who were endowed with bad conduct of body, speech, and mind, who reviled the noble ones, held wrong views, and undertook actions governed by wrong views—with the breakup of the body, after death, have reappeared in the plane of misery, the bad destinations, the lower realms, in hell. But these beings—who were endowed with good conduct of body, speech, and mind, who did not revile the noble ones, held right views, and undertook actions governed by right views—with the breakup of the body,

after death, have reappeared in the good destinations, in the heavenly world.' Thus with the divine eye, which is purified and surpasses the human, he sees beings passing away and reappearing—inferior and superior, beautiful and ugly, fortunate and unfortunate—and he understands how beings fare in accordance with their *kamma*.

98. "Great king, suppose in a central square there were a building with an upper terrace, and a man with keen sight standing there were to see people entering a house, leaving it, walking along the streets, and sitting in the central square. He would think to himself: 'Those people are entering the house, those are leaving it, those are walking along the streets, and those are sitting in the central square.' In the same way, great king, when his mind is thus concentrated, pure and bright … the *bhikkhu* directs and inclines it to the knowledge of the passing away and reappearance of beings. With the divine eye, which is purified and surpasses the human, he sees beings passing away and reappearing, and he understands how beings fare according to their *kamma*. This too, great king, is a visible fruit of recluseship more excellent and sublime than the previous ones.

The Knowledge of the Destruction of the Cankers

99. "When his mind is thus concentrated, pure and bright, unblemished, free from defects, malleable, wieldy, steady, and attained to imperturbability, he directs and inclines it to the knowledge of the destruction of the cankers. He understands as it really is: 'This is suffering.' He understands as it really is: 'This is the origin of suffering.' He understands as it really is: 'This is the cessation of suffering.' He understands as it really is: 'This is the way leading to the cessation of suffering.' He understands as it really is: 'These are the cankers.' He understands as it really is: 'This is the origin of the cankers.' He understands as it really is: 'This is the cessation of the cankers.' He understands as it really is: 'This is the way leading to the cessation of the cankers.'

"Knowing and seeing thus, his mind is liberated from the canker of sensual desire, from the canker of existence, and from the canker of ignorance. When it is liberated, the knowledge arises: 'It is liberated.' He understands: 'Destroyed is birth, the holy life has been lived, what had to be done has been done, there is nothing further beyond this.'

100. "Great king, suppose in a mountain glen there were a lake with clear water, limpid and unsullied. A man with keen sight, standing on the bank, would see oyster-shells, sand and pebbles, and shoals of fish moving about and keeping still. He would think to himself: 'This is a lake with clear water, limpid and unsullied, and there within it are oyster-shells, sand and pebbles, and shoals of fish moving about and keeping still.'

"In the same way, great king, when his mind is thus concentrated, pure and bright .... the *bhikkhu* directs and inclines it to the knowledge of the destruction of the cankers. He understands as it really is: 'This is suffering' ... He understands: 'Destroyed is birth, the holy life has been lived, what had to be done has been done, there is nothing further beyond this.' This too, great king, is a visible fruit of recluseship more excellent and sublime than the previous ones. And, great king, there is no other fruit of recluseship higher or more sublime than this one."

King Ajātasattu Declares Himself a Lay Follower

101. When the Exalted One had finished speaking, King Ajātasattu said to him: "Excellent, venerable sir! Excellent, venerable sir! Just as if one were to turn upright what had been turned upside down, or to reveal what was hidden, or to point out the right path to one who was lost, or to bring a lamp into a dark place so that those with keen sight could see forms, in the same way, venerable sir, the Exalted One has revealed the *Dhamma* in numerous ways. I go for refuge to the Exalted One, to the *Dhamma*, and to the *Bhikkhu Saṅgha*. Let the Exalted One accept me as a lay follower gone for refuge from this day onwards as long as I live.

"Venerable sir, a transgression overcame me. I was so foolish, so deluded, so unskillful that for the sake of rulership I took the life of my own father, a righteous man and a righteous king. Let the Exalted One acknowledge my transgression as a transgression for the sake of my restraint in the future."

102. "Indeed, great king, a transgression overcame you. You were so foolish, so deluded, so unskillful that for the sake of rulership you took the life of your father, a righteous man and a righteous king. But since you have seen your transgression as a transgression and make amends for it according to the *Dhamma*, we acknowledge it. For, great king, this is growth in the discipline of the Noble One: that a person sees his transgression as a transgression, makes amends for it according to the *Dhamma*, and achieves restraint in the future."

103. When this was said, King Ajātasattu said to the Exalted One: "Now, venerable sir, we must go. We have many tasks and duties."

"Do whatever seems fit, great king."

Then King Ajātasattu rejoiced in the word of the Exalted One and thanked him for it. Rising from his seat, he paid homage to the Exalted One, circumambulated him, and departed.

104. Soon after King Ajātasattu had left, the Exalted One addressed the *bhikkhus*: "This king, *bhikkhus*, has ruined himself; he has injured himself. *Bhikkhus*, if this king had not taken the

life of his father, a righteous man and a righteous king, then in this very seat there would have arisen in him the dust-free, stainless eye of *Dhamma*."

Thus spoke the Exalted One. Elated in mind, the *bhikkhus* rejoiced in the Exalted One's word.

Here ends the Sāmaññaphala Sutta

Part Two

The Commentarial Exegesis of the Sāmaññaphala Sutta

[Note: CY. = commentary; SUB.CY. = subcommentary; N.SUB.CY.= new subcommentary. The passage numbers of the exegetical sections correspond with those of the *sutta*. The explanation for any *sutta* statement commented on can be located by finding the corresponding passage number in the exegetical section. The comment on the statement is usually introduced by its key words; in most cases these cues are found in the commentary itself. Phrases in square brackets in the commentary have been supplied from the subcommentary or the new subcommentary, those in the subcommentary from the new subcommentary. English phrases in parenthesis are the translator's own additions.]

Statements of Ministers

1. In Jīvaka Komārabhacca's mango grove

CY. When it is said "the Exalted One was dwelling at Rājagaha, in Jīvaka Komārabhacca's Mango Grove," the meaning should be understood thus: he was living in Jīvaka Komārabhacca's Mango Grove which was near Rājagaha. The name "Jīvaka Komārabhacca" means 'a living person who has been raised by a prince.' For as a baby, he was found abandoned, surrounded by crows. When they saw that the baby was still living, they gave him the name Jīvaka. He was brought to the palace and nurtured by the royal nursemaids. Thus, as he was raised by the prince, they gave him the name Komārabhacca. The story of Jīvaka is related at length in the Khandhakas and explained in the *Samantapāsādikā*, the commentary to the *Vinaya*.[13]

Once, when the Exalted One's body was afflicted by a disorder of the humors, Jīvaka treated him with a purgative. He then gave the Buddha a pair of Siveyyaka cloths[14], and at the conclusion of the (Buddha's) thanksgiving talk for the cloths, he was established in the fruit of stream-entry. Thereupon he thought: "I should go to wait upon the Buddha two or three times a day, but the Bamboo Grove is too far away. My park, the Mango Grove, is closer. Let me build a dwelling there for the Exalted One." He set up night-quarters, day-quarters, caves, huts, pavilions, etc., built a Fragrant Cottage suitable for the Exalted One, and erected a copper-colored wall eighteen yards high surrounding the Mango Grove. He treated the *Saṅgha* of *bhikkhus* headed by the Buddha to an offering of a meal and robes, and after pouring the gift-water, presented the dwelling.

King Ajātasattu of Magadha

CY. The astrologers (who were consulted before his birth) predicted: "Even while he is as yet unborn (*ajāta*), he will be the king's enemy (*sattu*)"; thus (he was named) Ajātasattu, "unborn enemy."

It is said that when he was still in his mother's womb, the queen (his mother) developed the compulsive urge to drink blood from the king's right arm. She considered: "This compulsive urge that has arisen is terrible; I should not report it to anyone." Being unable to express it, she became thin and pale. The king asked her: "Dear, your body has become pallid. What is the reason?"—"Do not ask, great king."—"Dear, if you don't express your thoughts to me, to whom will you express them?" Urging her in

13. In the Mahāvagga (Vin I 268-80) it is related how Jīvaka, the abandoned son of a courtesan, was found and raised by Prince Abhaya, attended medical school at Taksilā, and eventually came to be appointed personal physician of the Buddha and the *Bhikkhu Saṅgha*. He had attained the fruit of stream-entry.

14. Hailing from the Sivi country, a kind of highly valuable cloth.

various ways, he convinced her to speak. Having heard, he said: "Dear, why do you regard this as terrible?" He then sent for his physician, had him make an incision in his arm with a golden knife, collected the blood in a golden vessel, mixed it with water, and made her drink it.

The astrologers, hearing this, declared: "This child in her womb will be the king's enemy. He will kill the king." The queen heard this and thought: "They say that when the child comes out from my belly he will kill the king." Wishing to have an abortion, she went to the park and had her belly trampled upon, but abortion did not take place. She went again and again and did the same thing. The king inquired: "Why do you go to the park so often?" Having learned the reason he said: "Dear, we do not even know whether you have a son or a daughter in your womb. If we do this to a child begotten by ourselves, a great calamity will appear in our land of India. Do not do so." Having thus dissuaded her, he set a guard over her. When the child took birth she thought: "I will kill him," but guards took the child away from her. Some time later, after the prince had attained to growth, they showed him to the queen. When she saw him, maternal affection arose within her and she could not have him killed. Eventually the king appointed his son viceroy.

One time Devadatta, while in seclusion, thought to himself: "Sāriputta has an assembly of followers, Mahāmoggallāna has an assembly of followers, Mahākassapa has an assembly of followers. Thus each of these maintains his own following. I, too, will gather a following." He considered: "It won't be possible to acquire an assembly without gain. So let me obtain gain." Then, as related in the Khandhakas, by means of the miracle of supernormal power he won the confidence of Prince Ajātasattu. The prince came to wait upon him morning and evening with five hundred chariots. Aware of his great trust, one day Devadatta approached the prince and said: "In the past, O prince, men lived long; now they are short-lived. Therefore, prince, you should kill your father and become the king, I will kill the Exalted One and become the Buddha." Thus he enjoined the prince to kill his father.

The prince thought: "Master Devadatta has great spiritual power. There is nothing he does not know." He fastened a dagger to his thigh and entered the inner palace in the middle of the day, but being fearful, apprehensive, alarmed and anxious, he muddled up the instructions he was given [by Devadatta] and the ministers arrested him and examined him. They disputed whether the prince should be killed along with Devadatta and all the *bhikkhus* [in Devadatta's assembly]. Deciding to do whatever the king commanded, they reported the matter to the king.

The king demoted those ministers who wanted to kill the prince and Devadatta, and promoted those ministers who did not want to kill them. He asked the prince: "Prince, why do you want to kill me?"—"I want your kingdom, your majesty." The king gave him his kingdom.

When the prince reported to Devadatta that his wish had been granted, Devadatta said: "Like a man who beats the kettledrums after caging a jackal, you imagine you have finished your work. Within a few days your father, considering the contempt you have shown him, will himself become king."—"Then what should I do, venerable sir?"—"Cut off the root. Kill him!"—"But isn't it true, venerable sir, that my father should not be killed by a weapon?"—"Then kill him by cutting off his food."

The prince had his father thrown into the torture chamber, a smokehouse built for the purpose of inflicting punishment. He said: "Do not let anyone see him except my mother." The queen put rice in a golden vessel and entered, bringing the vessel on her hip. The king ate the rice and continued to live. The prince asked him: "My father, how do you continue to live?" Having learned how, he ordered: "Do not let my mother enter bringing anything on her hip." From then on the queen entered putting the vessel in her topknot. Having learned about this, he ordered: "Do not let her enter with her hair bound in a topknot." Then she put rice inside a pair of golden shoes, sealed the shoes, put them on, and entered. In this way the king continued to live. Again, the prince asked how he lived, and having learned how, he ordered: "Do not let her enter wearing shoes." From then on the queen bathed with scented water, anointed her body with the four sweets [curd, honey, ghee, and molasses], dressed, and entered. The king continued to live by licking her body. Again the prince asked, and having heard the report, he ordered: "From now on prevent my mother from entering." The queen stood behind the door and cried out: "O, my husband Bimbisāra! You did not let me kill him in his infancy. You yourself nurtured your own enemy. This is the last time I will see you. From now on I will never see you again. If I have done anything wrong, please forgive me, my lord!" Weeping and wailing, she departed.

From then on the king did not receive any food, but continued to live by walking back and forth in the happiness of the path and fruit (of stream-entry).[15] His body became extremely radiant. The prince asked: "Father, how do you continue to live?" Learning that he continued to live by walking back and forth, and seeing that this body had become extremely radiant, the prince thought: "Now I will prevent him from walking back and forth." He ordered his barbers: "Cut open my father's feet with a razor, smear them with salt and oil and roast them over flameless coals of acacia wood."

When the king saw the barbers, he thought: "Someone must have informed my son; they have come to trim my beard." They went to him, bowed down before him, and stood up. He asked: "Why have you come here?" They reported their instructions. He said: "You should do what your king commands." They asked him to sit down, bowed to him, and said: "Your majesty, we are doing what the king has ordered us to do. Do not be angry at us. This isn't proper for a righteous king such as yourself." Then with the left hand they grabbed his ankles, with the right they took a razor, cut open his feet, smeared them with salt and oil, and roasted them over flameless coals of acacia wood. (Because of the torture) the king experienced severe pain. While recollecting the Buddha, the *Dhamma*, and the *Saṅgha* he withered up like a garland of flowers thrown upon the terrace of a *cetiya*, and was

15. The king had attained the path of stream-entry at the close of the first discourse he heard from the Buddha, when he met him soon after his Enlightenment.

reborn in the heavenly world of the Four Great Kings as a spirit named Janavasabha in the retinue of Vessavaṇa.[16]

That same day a son was born to Ajātasattu.[17] Two letters reached him simultaneously, one telling him of the birth of his son, the other of his father's death. The ministers, thinking: "First we will report to him the birth of his son," handed him that letter. The moment (he read the letter) love for his newborn son arose in the king, shook his entire body, and penetrated through to the marrow of his bones. At that moment he understood what it means to be a father. Realizing "When I was born my own father felt such love for me," he said: "Go, men, release my father." They said: "How can we release him, your majesty?" and handed him the other letter.

As soon as he learned the news, he went weeping to his mother and asked her: "Mother, did my father feel love for me when I was born?" She said: "Foolish son, what are you saying? When you were a child, you had a small boil on your finger. You kept on weeping and they couldn't quiet you down, so they took you to your father, who was sitting in the judgement hall. Your father put your finger in his mouth and the boil broke open right in his mouth. He couldn't spit out the pus and blood, so out of love for you, he swallowed them. Such was your father's love for you." Weeping and lamenting, he disposed of his father's body.

Devadatta then approached Ajātasattu and told the king to order some men to assassinate the Buddha. He sent the men given to him (but the plot failed). Then Devadatta ascended Vulture's Peak himself and with a sling hurled a rock at the Buddha (but this plan also failed). He even had the elephant Nālāgiri let loose (at the Buddha), but no matter what method he used, he could not kill the Exalted One. When his gains and honor had been lost, he

---

16. The ruler of the Yakkhas, whose kingdom lies in the northern quarter of the heaven of the Four Great Kings.

17. This could not have been Udāyibhadda., whose mother Vajirā, daughter of King Pasenadi, was given to Ajātasattu in marriage only later.

asked the Buddha to accept his five proposals.[18] The Buddha did not agree, and Devadatta thought to use those points to win over the people. He created a schism in the *Saṅgha*, but Sāriputta and Moggallāna went to his residence, won back his followers for the Buddha, and returned leading them away. When he learned this, he vomited hot blood.

For nine months Devadatta lay on the sickbed, after which he was filled with remorse. He asked: "Where is the Teacher now staying?" When they told him that the Buddha was staying at the Jetavana monastery, he said: "Then take me by my bed and let me see the Teacher." But because he had performed *kamma* which disqualified him from seeing the Exalted One, while he was being carried, right beside the lotus pond in the Jetavana monastery, the earth split open and he fell in and landed in the Great Hell. This is a brief account; a detailed account is related in the Khandhakas (Cullavagga, VII).

Thus the king was named Ajātasattu because the astrologers predicted: "Even while he is as yet unborn, he will be the king's enemy."

KING AJĀTASATTU WAS SITTING ON THE UPPER TERRACE OF HIS PALACE

CY. Why was the king sitting there? In order to ward off sleep. For, from the day he killed his father, whenever he went to bed, as soon as he closed his eyes he felt as if he had been struck by a hundred spears and woke up crying. When asked what the trouble was, he answered, "Nothing." Thus sleep became repugnant to him and he was sitting there in order to ward off sleep.

18. The five proposals: that the monks live exclusively in forests, not in town or villages; that they live solely beneath trees, not in shelters; that they wear only rag-robes, not prepared robes; that they live only on almsround, not on food presented by invitation; and that they refuse to eat meat or fish (Vin II 196–97).

THE KING UTTERED THE FOLLOWING JOYFUL EXCLAMATION

CY. As oil which cannot be contained in its barrel spills over and is called an oil slick; as water which cannot be contained in a tank inundates the land and is called a flood; so when the heart cannot contain a joyous statement, the statement becomes excessively strong and, unable to remain within, it comes out as speech. That is called a "joyful exclamation" (*udāna*).

WHAT RECLUSE OR BRAHMIN SHOULD WE VISIT TONIGHT?

CY. By this entire statement the king gives a hint. To whom does he give it? To Jīvaka. For what purpose? In order to see the Exalted One. But couldn't he go to the Exalted One on his own? No, he could not. Why? Because of his great crimes. For his own father, whom he had killed, was a noble disciple and a supporter of the Exalted One, and he himself had supported Devadatta, who had done much harm to the Exalted One. Thus he had committed great crimes, and because of these he could not go to the Exalted One on his own. But Jīvaka was a supporter of the Exalted One, so he gave him a hint, thinking: "I will see the Exalted One, (following Jīvaka) like his shadow."

Did Jīvaka understand that the king was giving him a hint? Yes, he understood. Then why did he remain silent? In order to avoid being interrupted. For he thought: "In this assembly there are present many who are supporters of the six teachers. Since the teachers on whom they attend are untrained, they themselves are not properly trained. If I should begin to speak about the virtues of the Exalted One, they would rise up, interrupt me, and speak about the virtues of their own teachers. Thus I would not be able to complete my talk on the virtues of the Teacher. But as the king has already approached the teachers whom they support, he will not be satisfied with their account of (their teachers') virtues, knowing such talk to be substanceless. Then he will question me. Without being interrupted, I will explain the virtues of the Teacher and take the king along with me to meet him." Thus, though he understood (the hint), he remained silent in order to avoid being interrupted.

The ministers thought: "Today the king extols the night in five ways. Surely he wishes to approach some recluse or brahmin, question him, and hear his *Dhamma*. He will show great honor to the (recluse or brahmin) whose *Dhamma* inspires his confidence. And it will be fortunate for the one whose recluse wins the support of the royal family." Having such aims in mind, each of the ministers thought: "I will praise the recluse I support and go taking the king along with me." Thus each one began to praise the recluse he personally supported.

2–7. The Six Teachers

(1) *Pūraṇa Kassapa*. Pūraṇa was the name of this teacher, Kassapa his clan. He was given the name Pūraṇa ("fulfilling"), it is said, because he was born into a family consisting of ninety-nine slaves, thus fulfilling the auspicious number (of a hundred). Because he was an auspicious slave, no one ever told him "This is well done" or "This is badly done," "This should be done" or "This has not been done." He thought to himself: "Why should I stay here?" and he fled. Thieves stole his clothes. Not knowing how to cover himself with leaves or grass, he entered a village naked. People saw him and thought: "This recluse is an *arahat*, with few wishes. There is no one like him." They approached him bringing cakes, rice, etc. From then on, even when he gained a cloak, he did not wear it, aware: "It is because I go about without clothes that I received this cloak." He took [his nakedness] as his going forth (*pabbajjā*). Various groups of five-hundred men went forth under him; thus it is said: "Pūraṇa Kassapa, the leader of an order" etc.

KING AJĀTASATTU REMAINED SILENT

CY. As a man wishing to eat a sweet, golden colored mango would become dissatisfied if a bitter *kājara* fruit were brought and placed in his hand, so the king, wishing to hear sweet *Dhamma* talk concerning such virtues as the *Jhānas* and modes of direct knowledge, and stamped with the three characteristics, now became extremely dissatisfied with this talk about the virtues of Pūraṇa, as he had previously seen this teacher and was dissatisfied with him even then. Thus he remained silent. Though dissatisfied, he remained silent and tolerated that talk, as displeasing as it was to him, for he realized: "If I scold that minister and order him to be grabbed by his neck and expelled, the others will become afraid that the same fate will befall them and no one will say anything." But since he remained silent, another minister, thinking, "I will praise the recluse I myself support," started to speak.

(2) *Makkhali Gosāla*. Makkhali was his (proper) name; his second name, Gosāla ("of the cowshed") derives from the fact that he was born in [the village of] Gosāla. [Others, however, say that he was born in a cowshed.] It is said that he was carrying a pot of oil across muddy ground when his master called out, "Do not stumble (*mā khali*), dear." Due to carelessness, he stumbled and fell. Afraid of his master, he started to flee. His master pursued him and grabbed the edge of his cloak. He discarded the cloak and fled without clothes. The rest is the same as in the story of Pūraṇa.

(3) *Ajita Kesakambala*. Ajita was his name, and he wore a hair-blanket (*kesakambala*). A hair-blanket is a blanket made out of human hair; there is no article of clothing more repulsive than that. As the Buddha says: "*Bhikkhus*, whatever woven articles of clothing there are, the hair-blanket is considered the most repulsive of these. A hair-blanket is cold in cold weather, hot in hot weather, ugly, foul-smelling, and uncomfortable to the touch." (AN 3:135/A I 286).

(4) *Pakudha Kaccāyana*. Pakudha was his name, Kaccāyana his clan. He refused to use cool water. Even after moving his bowels, he did not wash with cool water, but only with warm water or oil. If he passed through a river or a puddle of water on the path, he thought: "My moral discipline has been broken." He then re-established his moral discipline by building a mound of sand and continued on his way. He held the theory of bad luck (*nissirīka-laddhika*).

(5) *Sañjaya Belaṭṭhaputta*. His name was Sañjaya; he was the son (*putta*) of Belaṭṭha, thus Belaṭṭhaputta.

(6) *Nigaṇṭha Nātaputta.* He is called Nigaṇṭha ("knotless") because he proclaimed the doctrine: "We have no knots of defilements, no ties of defilements; we are free from the bonds of defilements." He was the son of Nāta, thus Nātaputta.

Jìvaka Komārabhacca's Statement

8. After hearing their statements the king thought to himself: "I do not wish to hear the statements of those who are speaking. I wish to hear the statement of that one who is keeping silent like a Supaṇṇa bird in the Nāga land. This isn't helpful to me." Then it occurred to him: "Jīvaka is a supporter of the Exalted Buddha, the peaceful one. He himself is peaceful. Therefore, like a *bhikkhu* endowed with vows, he sits silently. He will not speak unless I speak. The foot of the elephant must be grabbed while the elephant is trampling (on the trap)." Thus he himself took the initiative in consulting him and asked: "Friend Jīvaka, why do you keep silent? While each of these ministers praises the recluse he supports, you do not even open your mouth. Don't you support some recluse as they do? Are you poor? Didn't my father give you royalties? Or do you lack faith in anyone?"

Then Jīvaka thought: "The king wants me to speak about the virtues of the recluse I support. This is not the time for me to remain silent. I should not speak about the virtues of the Teacher in the way these ministers speak about the virtues of their recluses—by first bowing to the king and then sitting down." So he rose up from his seat, bowed down to the ground in the direction where the Exalted One was dwelling, lifted his hands to his head in reverential salutation, and said: "Great king, do not think that I approach any recluse indiscriminately. For when my Teacher took conception in the mother's womb, when he emerged from the womb, when he made his great renunciation, when he achieved Enlightenment, and when he set in motion the Wheel of the *Dhamma*, the ten-thousandfold world-system shook. So too, when he performed the Twin Miracle and when he descended from the heavenly worlds (after teaching the *Abhidhamma* there). I will speak about the virtues of the Teacher. Listen with a one-pointed mind, great king!" Having said this, he then began to speak: "Your majesty, he is the Exalted One, a worthy one, perfectly enlightened," etc.

When Jīvaka had finished explaining the meaning of each term he said: "Thus, great king, my Teacher is a worthy one; he is perfectly enlightened; … . he is exalted. Your majesty should visit the Exalted One. Perhaps if you visit him, he might bring peace to your mind." Speaking thus, he in effect says: "Great king, even when questioned by a hundred persons like yourself, or by a thousand such, or by a hundred thousand such, the Teacher has the power and ability to grasp their intentions and to answer them. You should approach him confidently, great king, and ask your question."

9. When the king heard this talk about the virtues of the Exalted One, his entire body was immediately suffused with the five grades of rapture.[19] At that very moment he became desirous to go to the Exalted One. Thinking, "If I am to go to the Buddha at this time there is no one apart from Jīvaka who can get the vehicles prepared quickly enough," he said: "Then get the elephant vehicles prepared, friend Jīvaka."

Among the many different kinds of vehicles, elephant vehicles are the best, and since one is going to see the best person, one should go in the best kind of vehicle. Moreover, horse vehicles and chariots, etc., are noisy and their sounds can be heard from the distance, but elephant vehicles proceed step by step and thus one does not hear any sound. Thinking that one should approach the peaceful, quiescent Exalted One in peaceful, quiet vehicles, the king ordered the elephant vehicles to be prepared.

Jīvaka undertook the preparations in the way described without being told to do so, simply through his prudence. For he thought: "The king says he is going at this time, and kings

---

19. *Pīti*. These are: momentary rapture, minor rapture, showering rapture, uplifting rapture, and pervading rapture (*Vism* IV. 94-99, pp. 149-50). Bhikkhu Ñāṇamoli renders *pīti* as happiness, which in this translation is reserved for *sukha*.

have many enemies. If some obstacle should arise along the way, people will blame me for taking the king out at an improper time. And they will blame the Exalted One for giving *Dhamma* talk without regard for the time. Therefore, I should arrange protection for the king, so that no one will blame either myself or the Exalted One."

Further, when supported by women, men do not become afraid. Thus, so that the king would go along happily surrounded by his women, Jīvaka arranged for five hundred female elephants to be prepared. He had five hundred of the king's women mounted on these, disguised as men, carrying swords and spears in their hands, surrounding the king. He further thought: "This king does not have the supporting conditions for gaining the paths and fruits in this present existence. The Buddhas explain the *Dhamma* when they have seen the supporting conditions (in their audience). So let me assemble a great multitude of people. For then the Teacher, having seen someone with the supporting conditions, will teach the *Dhamma*, and that will be beneficial to the multitude." So he sent out announcements here and there and had it proclaimed: "Today the king will go to see the Exalted One. Let everyone protect the king according to his means."

Jīvaka himself, having arranged the king's retinue, went along close to the king, thinking: "If any danger arises, I will be the first to give my own life for the sake of the king." But there were so many torches—hundreds and thousands beyond limit.

10. He was suddenly gripped by fear, etc.

CY. Herein, there are four kinds of fear: fear as mental anxiety (*citt'utrāsa-bhaya*), fear as knowledge (*ñāṇa-bhaya*), fear as a fearful object (*ārammaṇa-bhaya*), and fear as moral dread (*ottappa-bhaya*). Among these, fear as mental anxiety is referred to in the passage: "In dependence on birth there arises fear, fright," etc. Fear as knowledge has come down in the passage: "Those (gods), having heard the *Tathāgata*'s teaching of the *Dhamma*, generally fall into fear, a sense of urgency, and terror" (SN 22:78/S III 85). Fear as a fearful object is referred to in the passage: "Is this the fear and dread that is coming?" (MN 4/M I 21). Fear as moral dread is indicated in the passage: "In this they praise fear, not valor; for from fear the good do no evil" (SN 4:33/S I 21). Among these, here *fear as mental anxiety* is intended.

SUB. CY. Mental anxiety is itself fear in the sense of fearing. Fear as knowledge is the fear arisen when a fearful object (or situation) appears as fearful, and one scrutinizes it as fearful, knowing: "This is to be feared." Hence it is said: "But does the knowledge of appearance as terror [itself] fear or does it not fear? It does not fear. For it is simply the mere judgement that past formations have ceased, present ones are ceasing, and future ones will cease" (Vism XXI. 32, p.754). Fear as a fearful object is something from which fear arises. Moral dread is that by reason of which one fears doing evil.

CY. By why did the king become afraid? Because of the quietness he suspected Jīvaka and thus he became afraid. Jīvaka, it is said, had already informed the king in the upper terrace of the palace: "Great king, the Exalted One is fond of quietness. He should be approached quietly." Therefore the king prohibited the playing of musical instruments; the instruments were merely taken along. Also, they did not speak aloud, but went along giving signals with a snap of the fingers. In the Mango Grove not even the sound of sneezing was heard, and kings generally delight in sound. Because of the quietness he became uneasy, and the following suspicion arose in him regarding Jīvaka: "This Jīvaka told me there are 1250 *bhikkhus* in the Mango Grove, yet not even the sound of sneezing is heard here. He must be lying. Wishing to usurp the kingship for himself, he has deceived me, led me out of the city, set up an army in front, and is going to arrest me. For he has the strength of five elephants, and he is going along close beside me, and there is not even a single armed man near me. O, what harm has befallen me!" Having become so much afraid, he could not conduct himself fearlessly, but revealed his own fearfulness to Jīvaka.

Jīvaka thought: "This king does not know me; he does not know that Jīvaka does not take another's life. If I do not reassure him, he will perish." Thus, reassuring the king, he said: "Do not be afraid, great king," etc. He says "Go forward" twice, hurrying along, because if he had said this once it would not be firm. He points out the lights burning in the pavilion hall to show: "A group of thieves does not stay where lamps are burning. You should go where you see those lamps, great king."

Question on Fruits of Recluseship

11. As soon as the king dismounted from the elephant and set foot on the ground, the splendor of the Exalted One suffused his body. Immediately, his entire body broke out into a sweat and his clothes oppressed him, so that he felt as if they should be removed. He remembered his own crime and great fear arose in him. He could not go directly to the Exalted One, but took Jīvaka by the hand and walked around as if touring the monastery grounds, saying: "You have built this well, Jīvaka, you have built this well." Thus, praising the monastery, he gradually approached the door of the pavilion hall.

Why does he ask: "Where is the Exalted One?" Some say because he did not know. They say that in his youth he had seen the Exalted One when he came to him along with his father; but afterwards, as a result of associating with evil friends, he killed his father, sent assassins (to work for Devadatta), set the elephant Dhanapāla (Nālāgiri) loose (against the Buddha), and having thus become a great criminal, he did not meet the Exalted One face to face. Because of this, they say, he did not recognize him. But that is not the reason. For the Exalted One, sitting in the middle of the pavilion hall surrounded by the company of *bhikkhus*, appeared like the full moon surrounded by the host of stars. Marked with the most excellent bodily characteristics, adorned with the special features of physical beauty, he illuminated the entire monastery with his six-colored rays. Who would not have known him? The king asks this as a mannerism of sovereignty (*issariyalīlā*). For this is the nature of those of royal family; though knowing something, they ask as if they do not know. But Jīvaka, having heard this question, thought to himself: "This king, standing in front of the Buddha, asks, 'Where is the Exalted One?' This is as if someone standing on the earth were to ask, 'Where is the earth?'; or as if someone looking up at the sky were to ask, 'Where are the sun and moon?'; or as if someone standing at the foot of Mount Sineru were to ask, 'Where is Sineru?' I will show him the Exalted One." Making a reverential salutation towards the Exalted One, he said: "That is the Exalted One, great king," etc.

12. As the king surveyed the company of *bhikkhus*, wherever he looked the company sat in complete silence. Not even one *bhikkhu* was playing with his hands or feet or broke out into a cough. Not even one *bhikkhu* looked up at the king and his royal assembly standing in front of the Exalted One, or at the retinue of nautch-girls adorned with all their ornaments. All sat there, looking only at the Exalted One.

The king, gaining confidence (at the sight of) such peace, again and again surveyed the company of *bhikkhus* sitting there with calm faculties, like a clear lake free from mud. He then uttered his joyful exclamation: "May my son, the Prince Udāyibhadda, enjoy such peace as the company of *bhikkhus* now enjoys!" The meaning is: "May he enjoy the bodily, verbal, and mental peace, and the peaceful conduct, which the company of *bhikkhus* enjoys!" He did not say this intending: "O, may my son go forth (as a monk) and become peaceful like these *bhikkhus*!" Rather, having gained confidence seeing the company of *bhikkhus*, he remembered his son. For that is the nature of people in the world: when they have gained something rare or seen something wonderful, they remember their dear relatives and friends.

Moreover, he said this because he was apprehensive about his son and desired peace for him. For he thought: "My son will ask: 'My father is young. Where is my grandfather?' Hearing 'Your father killed him', he might think: 'Then I shall kill my father and rule the kingdom!' Thus, apprehensive about his son, he spoke thus desiring this peace for him. Yet though he said this, his son eventually killed him.

In that dynasty parricide took place in five generations. Ajātasattu killed Bimbisāra; Udāyi killed Ajātasattu; Udāyi was killed by his own son, Mahāmuṇḍika; Mahāmuṇḍika was killed by his son Anuruddha; and Anuruddha was killed by his son Nāgadāsa. But the citizens became angry and thinking, "These kings destroy their own lineage; what do we need them for?" they killed Nāgadāsa.

> DO YOUR THOUGHTS, GREAT KING, FOLLOW THE CALL OF YOUR AFFECTION?

CY. Why does the Exalted One say this? It is said that before the king uttered his exclamation, the Exalted One had thought: "The king, having come, stands here silent and speechless. What is he thinking?" Having read his mind, he reflected: "Being unable to converse with me, he surveys the company of *bhikkhus* and remembers his son. I will start a conversation with him." Therefore, immediately after the king uttered his joyful exclamation, the Exalted One spoke the above words. This is the meaning: "Great king, as rain water, falling upon the highlands, flows down to the plain, so as you survey the company of *bhikkhus*, your affection goes towards your son."

Thereupon the king thought: "O, how wonderful are the virtues of the Buddha! There is no one who has committed such crimes towards the Exalted One as I have. I killed his chief supporter (King Bimbisāra); I accepted the request of Devadatta and sent assassins to kill him; I released the elephant Nālāgiri against him; with my support Devadatta hurled a stone at him. The Buddha should not even open his mouth towards such a criminal as myself, yet he freely addresses me. O, the Exalted One is well-established in the characteristic of a stable one (*tādilakkhaṇa*) in five modes.[20] I should not abandon such a teacher and search for a teacher elsewhere." Filled with joy, addressing the Exalted One, he said: "Venerable sir, I love my son," etc.

---

20. N.Sub.Cy. quotes here a long passage from the Mahāniddesa on the five kinds of "stability" of the *arahat*. In brief, he is stable through his equanimity towards pleasure and pain, his renunciation of defilements, his crossing of the round of rebirths, his liberation of mind, and his acquisition of the various virtues mentioned in the suttas.

13. Knowing the king's eagerness to ask a question, the Exalted One says: "Ask whatever you wish to, great king." He invites him to ask, extending to him the invitation of an Omniscient One, (implying): "Ask whatever you wish to. It is no trouble for me to answer. I will answer everything." This invitation is not shared in common even with *paccekabuddha*s, chief disciples, and great disciples. For they do not say, "Ask whatever you wish to," but: "Having heard, we will try to answer." Buddhas, however, say, "Ask whatever you wish to," inviting spirits, kings, gods, recluses, brahmins, and wanderers with the invitation of an Omniscient One.

14. Elated that the Exalted One had invited him to ask with the invitation of an Omniscient One, the king asked his question on the visible fruits of recluseship. This is the purport of the king's question: "Is it possible to point out any visible fruit of recluseship similar to the visible fruits discerned for the various worldly crafts and enjoyed by those who live by these crafts?" Therefore, speaking in terms of those who live by those crafts, he refers to the various crafts.

"Fruit of recluseship" (*Sāmaññaphala*): in the ultimate sense, recluseship is the path, and the fruit of recluseship is the noble fruit. As it is said: "What, *bhikkhus*, is recluseship? It is this Noble Eightfold Path: right view … right concentration. And what are the fruits of recluseship? The fruits of stream-entry, of the once-returner, of the non-returner, and of *arahatship*" (SN 45:35/S V 25). The king, however, does not know about these. Thus, in the text below, he asks concerning (the fruits illustrated by) the examples of the slave and the farmer.

15. Do you remember, great king …?

CY. The Exalted One did not answer the question directly, but reflected: "These many royal ministers who have come here are disciples of other religious teachers. If I were to speak, explaining the negative and positive sides, they would complain: 'Our king has come here with great eagerness, yet from the time he arrived the recluse Gotama speaks only of the quarrels and controversies of recluses.' Thus they would not listen carefully to the *Dhamma*. But if the king were to speak, they won't be able to complain, since they must follow him; for in the world people follow those who are in power. So then, let me give the king the task (of explaining the doctrines of the six teachers)." Turning that task over to the king, he asks: "Do you remember, great king, ever asking other recluses and brahmins this question?"

IT IS NOT TROUBLESOME FOR ME, VENERABLE SIR

CY. The intention of the king's statement is this: "It is difficult to speak in the presence of those who pretend to be wise, for they find fault with every word and letter. But the genuine wise men, having heard one's statement, praise what is well-spoken; and when something is wrongly spoken, contradicting the meaning and phrasing of the scriptures, they correct it and reformulate it. And there is no genuine wise man equal to the Exalted One." Thus the king says: "It is not troublesome for me, venerable sir, when the Exalted One or anyone like him is present."

The Six Outside Teachers and their Doctrines

1. Pūraṇa Kassapa

17. If one acts ... one does no evil

CY. He explains: "Even though a person does something with the idea 'I am doing evil,' evil is not done. There is no evil. Beings (simply) have the idea 'We are doing evil.' "

N. SUB. CY. "With the idea 'I am doing evil' ": by this he (Pūraṇa) indicates the presence of volition. Hence he shows: "Even for one who acts intentionally no evil is done, not to speak of one who acts unintentionally." "He does no evil" because it is impossible to arouse something previously nonexistent. Hence he says: "There is no evil."

His opponents object to his doctrine with the question: "If that is so (i.e. there is no evil) how is it that beings behave badly?" Wishing to counter this objection, Pūraṇa shows: "Beings (simply) have the idea: 'We are doing evil.' The doing of evil is a mere idea; there is no evil."

SUB. CY. This is meant (as the philosophical underpinning of Pūraṇa's ethical nihilism): "Causing harm and injury, etc., to living beings does not affect the self, since the self is permanent and immutable. The body is devoid of consciousness, like a block of wood, so even when it is destroyed no evil is done."

No outcome (of evil or merit)

CY. "Outcome" (*āgama*) is occurrence. In every case he rejects the doing of evil and of merit.

N. SUB. CY. When one acts, there is produced in one's mental continuum a condition for the production of the (corresponding) fruit. Thus the complete statement of the doctrine of the inefficacy of action asserts: "There is no *kamma* and no fruit of *kamma*." For if there were to be fruit of *kamma*, how could *kamma* be without any efficacy?

"In every case he rejects the doing of evil and of merit": the purport is that he does not explain the visible fruits of recluseship asked about by the king. This ascertainment has the purpose of indicating his rejection of the results (of *kamma*). For one who rejects *kamma* by implication also rejects results.

2. Makkhali Gosāla

19. THERE IS NO CAUSE OR CONDITION FOR THE DEFILEMENT OF BEINGS ... FOR THE PURIFICATION OF BEINGS

CY. By both words (cause, *hetu*, and condition, *paccaya*), he rejects the real condition for defilement, i.e. wrong bodily conduct, etc., and the real condition for purification, i.e. right bodily conduct, etc.

THERE IS NO SELF-DETERMINATION

CY. "Self-determination" (*attakāra*) is the *kamma* beings do on their own, by reason of which they attain the state of a god, the state of Māra, the state of Brahmā, the enlightenment of a disciple, the enlightenment of a *paccekabuddha*, or the omniscience (of a Buddha). This he rejects.

"Determination by others" (*parakāra*) is the exhortation and instruction given by others, in dependence upon which all people, except for the Great Beings (i.e. the *bodhisattas*), attain (the various desirable states) ranging from good fortune in the human state up to *arahatship*. He rejects this determination by others. Thus this fool strikes a blow at the Wheel of the Conqueror.

N. SUB. CY. The exception for the Great Beings is made because they are not dependent on determination by others (for their attainment of) the supramundane states. But there is (determination by others) in regard to mundane states, as our *Bodhisatta* gained the five modes of direct knowledge and the mundane meditative attainments in dependence on Ālāra and Uddaka (MN 26/M I 163-66). And (the commentator's statement) refers to the Great Beings in their last existence. *Paccekabodhisattas* should also be included here, since in their case too there is no determination (by others in regard to their supramundane attainments).

The "Wheel of the Conqueror" is the Buddha's teaching, which explains the existence of *kamma* and its fruits. He "strikes a blow" at it by rejecting the doctrines of *kamma* and the efficacy of action.

CY. "No personal determination" (*purisakāra*): he rejects the personal determination through which beings attain the aforementioned kinds of success. "No power" (*bala*): he denies that beings can establish themselves upon their own power, arouse their energy, and attain success. The terms "energy," "personal strength," and "personal fortitude" are synonymous with personal determination. They are brought in separately in order to reject the claim: "This has occurred through our energy, personal strength, and personal fortitude."

ALL SENTIENT BEINGS ... DEVOID OF ENERGY

CY. "All sentient beings" (*sabbe sattā*): he includes camels, oxen, donkeys, etc., without exception. "All living beings" (*sabbe pāṇā*): he says this with reference to creatures having one or two faculties. "All creatures" (*sabbe bhūtā*): this refers to beings born from eggs or from the womb. "All souls" (*sabbe jīvā*): this refers to rice, barley, wheat, etc.; because they undergo growth, he regards them as having souls. "Are helpless, powerless, devoid of energy": they have no self-control, power, or energy.

UNDERGOING TRANSFORMATION BY DESTINY, CIRCUMSTANCE, AND NATURE, THEY EXPERIENCE PLEASURE AND PAIN IN THE SIX CLASSES OF MEN

N. SUB. CY. Destiny (*niyati*) is predestination (*niyamanā*), that is, the fixity in realm of rebirth, social class, bondage and liberation, determined by the necessary sequence of events, which is like a row of unbreakable jewels strung along an uncuttable thread.

CY. "Circumstance" (*saṅgati*): going here and there among the six classes of men.

N. SUB. CY. The encounter with the totality, the going to those who are related among the six classes of men; going here and there among the different kinds of birth.

CY. "Nature" (*bhāva*): the inner nature (*sabhāva*).[21]

SUB. CY. He maintains that the whole world is transformed in various ways, without causes or conditions, spontaneously, solely by its own intrinsic nature, analogously to the sharpness of thorns, the roundness of wood apples, and the different shapes of animals and birds.

CY. By this whole statement Makkhali Gosāla shows: "Thus (all sentient beings) are transformed and achieve diversity due to destiny, circumstance, and nature. Whatever will be will be; whatever will not be will not be."

"The six classes of men" (*cha abhijāti*): abiding in the six classes of men, they experience pleasure and pain. He shows that there is no other plane of pleasure and pain.

THERE ARE FOURTEEN HUNDRED THOUSAND PRINCIPAL MODES OF ORIGIN (*YONIPAMUKHA*)

CY. The principal modes of origin are the highest modes of origin.[22]

N. SUB. CY. Among human beings, nobles, and brahmins, etc., are the primary modes of origin; among animals, lions and tigers, etc., are primary.

CY. "Five hundred kinds of *kamma*": he explains a senseless view devised solely by mere reasoning. The same principle applies in the case of five kinds of *kamma*, three kinds of *kamma*, etc. But some say: "He speaks of five kinds of *kamma* by way of the five sense faculties and three kinds by way of bodily (verbal, and mental) *kamma*."

---

21. Although the three determinants in Makkhali's system are obscure, we might conjecture that if *niyati* is destiny, then *saṅgati* and *bhāva* would be respectively the outer set of circumstances and the inner nature by which destiny controls the fortune of each individual.

22. Basham takes this category to refer to the total number of species of living beings in the universe, through which the transmigrating soul must pass before attaining emancipation . (*History and Doctrines of the Ājīvikas,* p. 241)

SUB. CY. "By mere reasoning": since the rationalists lack a hook [for grasping the real meaning] they conceive their mental constructions to be real and, adhering to them, grasp their assumption of rationalistic views. For this reason the wise do not have to examine each specific case of their views.

CY. "Full *kamma* and half-*kamma*": here his theory is that bodily and verbal *kamma* are full *kamma* and mental *kamma* is half-*kamma*.

SUB. CY. His theory is that the former two, because they are gross, are full *kamma*, while mental *kamma*, because it is subtle, is half-*kamma*.[23]

CY. "Sixty-two pathways": [Not knowing the natural language correctly] he speaks of sixty-two pathways as *dvaṭṭhipaṭipadā* [when it should be] *dvāsaṭṭhipaṭipadā*.[24]

"Sixty-two sub-aeons" (*antarakappā*): in a single great aeon there are sixty-four sub-aeons, but since he does not know about two of these, he says (that there are sixty-two).

SIX CLASSES OF MEN (*CHA ABHIJĀTIYO*)

CY. He declares that there are six classes of men: the black, the blue, the red, the yellow, the white, and the ultimate white.[25]

(1) CY. The black class (*kaṇhābhijāti*) is made up of butchers, hunters, fishermen, thieves, executioners, prison wardens, and those in other cruel lines of work.

(2) CY. The blue class (*nīlābhijāti*) is made up of *bhikkhus*. For *bhikkhus*, he says, eat having thrown thorns into the four requisites (robes, food, lodgings, and medicines). His own

---

23. It should be noted that Makkhali's conception of *kamma* could not admit the factor of free volition or intention, the primary aspect of *kamma* in the Buddhist conception.

24. Basham thinks these may be religious systems which every transmigrating soul must eventually pass through.

25. Essentially the same explanations of these categories as those given by Buddhaghosa are to be found at AN6:57/A III 383-84, where the classification is ascribed to Pūraṇa Kassapa. Significantly, there the blue class is said to include all recluses who affirm the moral efficacy of action.

canonical text says: "*Bhikkhus* have thorny behavior" (*bhikkhū kaṇṭakavuttikā*).

SUB. CY. By "*bhikkhus*" he means *bhikkhus* in the Buddha's dispensation. He says: "They eat having thrown thorns into the four requisites," intending that they use the requisites with desire and lust.

N. SUB. CY. The "thorns" are desire and lust, and "having thrown thorns in" is using the requisites fettered by desire and lust.

SUB. CY. Why does he say this? He makes the false assumption that *bhikkhus* use the most excellent requisites. Therefore, even though *bhikkhus* use requisites that have been righteously gained, he says "they eat having thrown thorns into the requisites," since this is contrary to the creed of the Ājīvikas.

CY. Or alternatively, he says that some who have gone forth have thorny behavior.

SUB. CY. That is, some [non-Buddhists] who have gone forth are especially devoted to indulging in self-mortification; thus they are living, as it were, on thorns.

(3) CY. The red class (*lohitābhijāti*) is made up of the one-robed he Nigaṇṭhas (Jains); for these are purer than the former two.

SUB. CY. They are purer because they undertake such observances as fasting and non-bathing.

(4) CY. The yellow class (*haliddābhijāti*) is made up of the white-clothed lay disciples of the naked ascetics. Thus he makes his own lay supporters superior even to the Nigaṇṭhas.

SUB. CY. The naked ascetics (*acelakā*) are the Ājīvikas; they are superior, according to the Ājīvikas' theory, because they are purer in mind.

(5) CY. The white class (*sukkābhijāti*) comprises the male, and female Ājīvikas: for these, he says, are purer than the previous four.

(6) CY. The ultimate white class (*paramasukkābhijāti*) is made up of Nanda Vaccha, Kisa Saṅkiccha, and Makkhali Gosāla; for they are the purest of all.

SUB. CY. For they have reached the peak in the special

practices of the Ājīvikas. Therefore they are the ultimate white class, purer than the Nigaṇṭhas, the Ājīvikas, and their lay disciples.

Eight stages in the life of man (*Aṭṭha purisabhūmiyo*)

CY. He declares that there are eight stages in the life of man:

(1) the stage of feebleness; (2) the stage of play; (3) the stage of learning to walk; (4) the erect stage; (5) the stage of training; (6) the recluse stage; (7) the conqueror stage; and (8) the prostrate stage.

(1) The stage of feebleness (*mandabhūmi*): this lasts for seven days following the day of birth; for after coming out from the womb beings are feeble and dull.

(2) The stage of play (*khiddābhūmi*): those who have come from an evil destination often cry and howl; those who come from a good destination remember it and laugh.

(3) The stage of learning to walk (*padavīmaṃsabhūmi*): this is the stage when the child takes hold of its parents' hands or feet, or a bed or chair, and places its feet on the ground.

(4) The erect stage (*ujugatabhūmi*): this is the stage when it is able to walk on its feet.

(5) The stage of training (*sekhabhūmi*): this is the stage when one has been trained in a craft.

(6) The recluse stage (*samaṇabhūmi*): this is the time when one has renounced the household life and gone forth (as an ascetic).

(7) The conqueror stage (*jinabhūmi*): this is the time when, having served a teacher, one knows.

(8) The prostrate stage (*pannabhūmi*): this is the stage of a *bhikkhu*, a prostrate one, a conqueror, one who does not say anything, a recluse without gains.

SUB. CY. The words "*bhikkhu*," "prostrate one" (*pannaka*), etc., are used in their own canonical texts. A prostrate one is one who wanders for almsfood, or one who is practicing (*paṭipannaka*) their own way of practice.

"A conqueror" (*jina*) is one who is old (*jiṇṇa*), low in vitality due to ageing, or one who abides having conquered the obstacles to his own practice. Such a one, it is said, does not speak to anyone, not even about his doctrine; thus he "does not say anything." But others explain that even when he is insulted by being called a camel, etc., he does not say anything (in reply) but bears it patiently.

He is "without gains" (*alābhī*) because he does not gain things by reason of his vows, stated thus: "He does not receive from the mouth of a pot," etc. (MN 51/M I 342). Thus, overcome by hunger and weakness, he ends up lying flat. This is declared to be a recluse in the prostrate stage.

THIRTY-SIX REALMS OF DUST, ETC.

CY. "Thirty-six realms of dust": places where dust accumulates; he says this referring to the backs of the hands, bottom of the feet, etc.[26]

"Seven spheres of percipient beings": he says this referring to camels, oxen, donkeys, goats, cattle, deer, and buffaloes. "Seven spheres of non-percipient beings": he says this referring to rice, paddy, barley, wheat, millet, beans, and *kadrūsaka*. "Seven kinds of jointed plants": plants grown from joints; he refers to sugarcane, bamboo, reeds, etc.

"Seven kinds of gods": there are many kinds of gods, but he says there are seven. Human beings, too, are of infinite kinds, but he says there are seven. "Seven kinds of demons" (*pisācā*): there are numerous kinds of demons, but he says there are seven. "Seven great lakes": he says this mentioning the Kaṇṇamuṇḍa, Rathakāra, Anotatta, Sīhappapāta, Chaddanta, Mandākiṇī, and Kuṇāladaha.

EIGHTY-FOUR HUNDRED THOUSAND GREAT AEONS

CY. He describes the duration of a great aeon as the time

26. Basham suggests that the "realms of dust" (*rajodhātu*) may be "elements of impurity" or passions which keep the souls in bondage (p.248).

it would take to drain a single great lake seven times by removing a single drop of water with the tip of a blade of *kusa*-grass once every hundred years. His theory asserts that when eighty-four hundred thousand of such great aeons have passed, the foolish and the wise make an end to suffering. The wise man, he says, cannot purify himself before this and the fool does not continue on beyond.

SUB. CY. Why not? Because that is the fixed time limit for the wandering on of beings (in *saṃsāra*).

BY THIS MORAL DISCIPLINE, ETC.

CY. By this moral discipline of the naked ascetics or by any other. "Observance" should be understood similarly. That the one who considers himself a wise man should "ripen unripened *kamma*" or "eliminate ripened *kamma* whenever it comes up," i.e. that he should purify himself beforehand, or that the one who considers himself a fool should continue on beyond the time stated to be the limits (to *saṃsāra*)—"that cannot be," i.e. neither is able to do that. "*Saṃsāra*'s limits … . can neither be shortened nor extended": *saṃsāra* is not shortened for the wise man, nor extended for the fool.

3. Ajita Kesakambala

22. THERE IS NO GIVING

CY. He says this intending that there are no fruits of giving, offering, and liberality.

THERE IS NO PRESENT WORLD, NO WORLD BEYOND

CY. For one living in the world beyond, this world does not exist, and for one living in this world, the world beyond does not exist. He shows: all are annihilated just where they are.

SUB. CY. For one living in the world beyond, there is no present world to be gained through *kamma*, and for one living in the present world, there is no world beyond to be gained through *kamma*.

"All are annihilated just where they are": whatever state of existence, mode of origin, etc., they live in, there they are annihilated; they perish without arising (elsewhere).

NO MOTHER, NO FATHER

CY. He says this intending that there are no fruits of right and wrong conduct towards parents.

NO BEINGS WHO HAVE TAKEN REBIRTH (*SATTĀ OPAPĀTIKĀ*)

CY. He says there are no beings who, having passed away, reappear (by way of rebirth).

SUB. CY. He shows: "The arising of these beings is entirely like that of a bubble. They do not come here after previously passing away."

THE EARTH (IN HIS BODY) RETURNS TO AND MERGES WITH THE (EXTERNAL) BODY OF EARTH

CY. The internal earth element (returns to and merges with) the external earth element. The same method with the other elements.

SUB. CY. One portion of the external body of earth has come and taken shape as a sentient being by becoming part of his internal (physical organism). Now that earth element, like the earth composing a pot, etc., returns to and merges with the external body of earth; it becomes united with it completely and indistinguishably.

"The same method with the other elements": that is, as the water, taken up from the great ocean by a rain cloud, becomes rain water and returns to and merges with the ocean; as a bolt of lightning, the splendor of which is taken from the sunlight, returns to and merges with the sunlight; and as a gust of wind segregated from the mass of air, returns to and merges with the mass of air (—so too with the elements of the body). That is the purport of this theorist.

HIS SENSE FACULTIES PASS OVER INTO SPACE

CY. The six sense faculties, including mind, enter space.

HIS MERITORIOUS OFFERINGS END IN ASHES

CY. The meaning is: "The gifts he gave, such as presents, gifts of honor, etc., all terminate in ashes. They do not go beyond, yielding fruit."

THE PRACTICE OF GIVING IS A DOCTRINE OF FOOLS

CY. He shows: "Fools prescribe giving, not the wise. Fools give, the wise take."

An overview of the three doctrines

CY. Among these, *Pūraṇa*, with his statement "By doing so there is no evil," denies *kamma* [because of his doctrine of the inefficacy of action]. *Ajita*, with his statement "One is annihilated with the breakup of the body," denies kammic results [because he completely rejects a future re-arising]. *Makkhali*, with his statement "There is no cause," etc., denies both.

SUB. CY. (He denies both) because by completely denying the cause, the fruit also is rejected. When he asserts "Beings are defiled and purified without any cause or condition," his assertion of the conditionless nature of defilement and purification rejects the result as much as it rejects *kamma*; thus he denies both *kamma* and its result.

CY. By denying *kamma* one denies its result [because there is no result when there is no *kamma*]. By denying the result one denies *kamma* [because when there is no result, *kamma* becomes inefficacious]. Thus all these thinkers, by denying both (*kamma* and its results), in effect espouse acausalism (*ahetukavāda*), the inefficacy of action (*akiriyavāda*), and moral nihilism (*natthikavāda*).

SUB. CY. Although these three theorists have come down separately in the texts by way of the explanation of their individual views, they all deny both (*kamma* and its result); and by denying both, they all expound acausalism, etc. For the moral nihilist, espousing annihilationism by his denial of the result, in effect expounds the inefficacy of action by his denial of *kamma* and acausalism by his denial of both. The same method with the other two.

CY. When people accept these theories and then recite and investigate them while sitting in their day-quarters or night-quarters, wrong mindfulness becomes established, taking as object (one of the three views): "No evil is done," or "There is no cause or condition," or "The dead are annihilated." The mind becomes one-pointed. The impulsions run their course.[27] At the first impulsion these people are curable; and so too at the second, etc. But at the seventh they cannot be cured even by the Buddhas; they cannot be turned back.

Someone might espouse one view among these three, another two, another three. But whether one espouses one, two, or three views, one adopts a wrong view with fixed consequences. One has met an obstruction to the path to heaven and an obstruction to the path to liberation. It is impossible for him to reach heaven immediately following this present existence, much less to reach liberation. This being has become a stump in the round of existence, a watchman of the earth.[28] Generally, one like this does not emerge from existence.

> Therefore a person with discernment
> Desirous of his spiritual growth
> Should keep far away from such harmful people
> As one would avoid a venomous snake.

SUB. CY. "Wrong mindfulness becomes established" (*micchāsati santiṭṭhati*): wrong mindfulness is the craving associated with the theory, and it is this which becomes

---

27. The *javana* or impulsion phase in the Abhidhammic account of the process of consciousness is the phase at which the mind originates its kammically determinate actions. This phase, according to the *Abhidhamma*, consists of seven occasions of *javana* consciousness.

28. The phrases "a stump in the round" (*vaṭṭakhāṇu*) and "watchman of the earth" (*paṭhavigopaka*) are probably intended to suggest that such a person remains stuck in *saṃsāra*, hindered by his wrong view even from finding the path to liberation.

established. For through oral tradition one first apprehends the general meaning of the view "by doing so there is no evil," etc. One then ponders that meaning with various reasons until it appears as cogent to the mind as if it possessed concrete form. By becoming accustomed to such a view over a long period of time, one arrives at a reflective acquiescence in it, thinking "It is true." When, again and again, one habitually indulges in and cultivates the view that has been accepted as true through reflective acquiescence, wrong thought directs craving to that view, with wrong effort reinforcing the craving; thus one apprehends things as having a nature which they do not really have. Thus it is the craving associated with the theory that is called wrong mindfulness.

"The mind becomes one-pointed": by gaining such particular conditions as applied thought, etc., the mind becomes steadied on its object; it abandons diffuseness and becomes one-pointed, as if absorbed. "Wrong concentration" (*micchā-samādhi*) is spoken of under the heading of "mind." For that concentration, gaining the power of the development through special conditions, performs the function of pervertedly concentrating the mind on its object, as in the case of sharpshooting archers, etc.

"The impulsions run their course" (*javanāni javanti*): after the preliminary series of impulsions have occurred in that mode a number of times, in the last series of impulsions [which forms the conviction in the truth of the view] seven impulsions run their course. "At the first impulsion they are curable," etc.: this simply shows the intrinsic nature of things. For at that moment no one is capable of curing them.

N. SUB. CY. (They cannot be cured) because, while they are standing in those states of impulsion, it is impossible to prevent the arising of the seventh impulsion. Thus the process of consciousness occurs so quickly that it is impossible to cure them (at that moment) by means of exhortation and instruction. Thus the commentator says: "They cannot be cured even by the Buddhas."[29]

---

29. These remarks refer to the fixity in the sequence of *javanas* within

SUB. CY. "Someone might espouse one view," etc.: someone who adheres to and habitually indulges in only one view espouses only one view. Those who adhere to and habitually indulge in two or three views espouse two or three views. By this statement the commentator shows that the entire preceding discussion of these views, which defined and explained them in terms of their common denial of both (*kamma* and result), was only a preliminary. But when (the adoption of a particular view) leads one into the fixed course of wrongness,[30] that view is not combined with other views; since it is established through its own colligation of conditions, it does not arise together with (other views) just as the distinguished achievements (the *Jhānas*, etc.) do not arise simultaneously with different objects.

"But whether one espouses one, two, or three views": by this the commentator shows that the three views have the same strength and yield the same fruit [that is, they obstruct the attainment of heaven (and the noble path)]. Therefore, though the three views arise in a single person uncombined, when one yields its results the other two lend their strength to it.

"A stump in the round": this statement is one whose meaning requires interpretation (*neyyattha*), not one whose meaning is explicit (*nītattha*). Thus in the *Papañcasūdanī* (the commentary to the *Majjhima Nikāya*) it is said: "Is his future (as a result of his wrong view) fixed only with regard to a single existence (the next one) or also with regard to subsequent existences? It is fixed only with regard to a single existence (the next one). But because he repeatedly indulges in that view, he will approve

their series and do not mean that the person cannot be led away from his wrong views at a later time.

30. The "fixed course of wrongness" (*micchattaniyāma*) is a course of unwholesome *kamma* strong enough to determine an unfortunate rebirth in the immediately following existence. The point of this discussion is that although a theorist may at different times adopt all three of the wrong views being expounded, when he adopts any view firmly enough to constitute a descent into the course of wrongness, the object of his adherence can only be a single one among the three views and not two or three together.

of the same view in subsequent existences too" (M-a 3:85). Since the unwholesome is feeble and powerless, not strong and powerful like the wholesome, the wrong view is said to be fixed only with regard to a single existence (the next one). Otherwise, the fixed course of wrongness would be absolutely final like the fixed course of rightness,[31] but it is not absolutely final.

Query: If so, then how can the expression "a stump in the round" be applied (to the one who adopts such views)?

Reply: Because he habitually indulges (in that view). As in the *Aṅguttara Nikāya* it is said: "The fool who has sunk down even once is sunken indeed" (AN 7:15/IV 11), so here the expression "a stump in the round" is used in the same way. For he espouses such a view because of certain conditions; thence it cannot be denied that sometimes, because of the opposite conditions, he may manage to emerge from that view. Therefore, in the commentary it is said: "*Generally* one like this does not emerge from existence."

N. SUB. CY. The statement ("This being has become a stump in the round of existence") is one whose meaning requires interpretation, and not one whose meaning is explicit, because the meaning has to be indicated by explaining: "He becomes 'a stump in the round' because generally one like this does not emerge from existence, since by habitually indulging in this or that view he approves of the same view in a subsequent existence too." But it must be added that he does not become "a stump in the round" in the sense that the fixed course of wrongness is absolutely final.

---

31. The fixed course of rightness (*sammattaniyāma*) is the Noble Eightfold Path. The firm adoption of any of the three wrong views has fixed consequences only for the next existence, but cannot cause permanent bondage to *saṃsāra*; in this it contrasts with the path, which can bring complete and irreversible liberation from *saṃsāra*.

4. Pakudha Kaccāyana

25. Unmade, unfashioned (*akaṭā, akaṭavidhā*)

SUB. CY. "Unmade" means that they are not made, not fashioned, by any cause, whether of a similar or dissimilar nature.

CY. "Unfashioned" means that they have not been constructed by anyone who commands them to be made.

SUB. CY. That is, there is no order or rule for their making. By both terms ("unmade" and "unfashioned") he shows that the seven bodies are not produced by any cause or condition in the world.

Uncreated, without a creator (*animmitā animmātā*)

CY. "Uncreated": not created by supernormal power.

SUB. CY. Not created by the supernormal power of some powerful god (*deva*) who has attained mastery of the mind, and not created by the supernormal power of a creator God (*issara*), etc.

Barren, stable as a mountain peak, standing firm like a pillar

SUB. CY. "Barren" (*vañjā*): they are fruitless, like barren cattle, barren palm trees, etc.; they are not productive of anything. By this statement he rejects the idea that the earth-body, etc., produce such things as visible forms, etc. For in his theory visible forms, sounds, etc., occur independently of the earth-body, etc.

"Stable as a mountain peak" (*kūṭaṭṭhā*): the intention is that these are not produced by anything and do not themselves produce anything, just like a mountain peak.

"Standing firm like a pillar" (*esikaṭṭhāyiṭṭhitā*): (he maintains that) when it is said, "The sprout, etc., are produced from the seed," the sprout which comes forth from the seed is already existing, not one which was not already existing; otherwise the consequence would follow that one thing is produced from something (absolutely) different.[32] [The same holds with regard to these seven bodies.]

THEY DO NOT ALTER, DO NOT CHANGE (*NA IÑJANTI NA VIPARIṆĀMENTI*)

CY. Because they are steady, standing firm like a pillar, "they do not alter," i.e. do not undergo transmutation, and "do not change," i.e. do not abandon their original nature.

DO NOT OBSTRUCT ONE ANOTHER (*NA AÑÑAMAÑÑAṀ BYĀBĀDHENTI*)

SUB. CY. Because their nature is unchangeable, they do not obstruct one another. If they were capable of undergoing transmutation, they would obstruct one another. Also, since they are incapable of assisting one another, they do not assist one another. To show this the text says: "They are incapable of causing one another pleasure or pain," etc.

THE BODY OF EARTH, ETC.

CY. The body of earth is the earth itself, or the assemblage of earth [because earth is one part of the body].

THERE IS NO KILLER, ETC.

CY. Just as, when one strikes a heap of beans with a sword, the sword enters in between the beans, so (in the apparent act of killing) the sword enters the space, the interstice, between the seven bodies. Therein he shows: (When one thinks) "I am taking his life," that is only a mere idea.

SUB. CY. Since the seven bodies are permanent and immutable, there can be no killing, and no causing of killing; hence there is no killer nor one who causes killing. Because the seven bodies are indestructible, there is, in the ultimate sense, no killing or causing of killing, etc.

---

32. For a full examination of this view, see *The All-Embracing Net of Views*, pp. 137–39.

5. Nigaṇṭha Nātaputta

28. A *NIGAṆṬHA* IS RESTRAINED WITH REGARD TO ALL WATER, ETC.

CY. "Restrained with regard to all water" (*sabbavārivārito*): he rejects the use of all cold water. It is said that he perceives sentient beings in cold water and thus does not use it.

SUB. CY. "He is endowed with the avoidance of all evil" (*sabbavāriyutto*): he is endowed with the characteristic of restraint from all modes (of evil).

"He is cleansed by the avoidance of all evil" (*sabbavāridhuto*): he has shaken off evil by the avoidance of all evil, characterized as the wearing away (of evil).

"He is suffused with the avoidance of all evil" (*sabbavāriphuto*): he is suffused with the avoidance of all evil, characterized as the destruction of *kamma* through the attainment of liberation by destroying the eight kinds of *kamma*.

HE IS CALLED A KNOTLESS ONE WHO IS SELF-PERFECTED, ETC.

CY. "Self-perfected" (*gatatto*): one whose mind has attained the peak.

SUB. CY. His mind has attained the highest bounds through the achievement of liberation.

CY. "Self-controlled" (*yatatto*): one who has subdued his mind.

SUB. CY. He has subdued his mind because there is nothing among the faculties such as the body, etc., to be subdued.

CY. "Self-established" (*ṭhitatto*): one whose mind is well-established. In his doctrine there is something that accords with the Buddha's teaching; but because his theory is not pure, it is all counted as (wrong) view.

SUB. CY. What accords with the Buddha's teaching is endowment with the avoidance of evil. The impure theory is his assertion: "There is a soul; it may be permanent, it may be impermanent," etc.

"It is all counted as (wrong) view": all the points he acquiesces in through reflection—(his teachings on) *kamma*, nature, the analysis, etc.—are counted as wrong view.

6. Sañjaya Belaṭṭhaputta

CY. The doctrine of Sañjaya is explained by the method stated in the section on "doctrines of endless equivocation" (*amarā-vikkhepavāda*) in the commentary to the *Brahmajāla Sutta*.[33]

First Two Visible Fruits

33. So, VENERABLE SIR, I ASK THE EXALTED ONE

CY. The meaning is: "Just as one cannot obtain oil by grinding sand, so I did not obtain anything essential from the doctrines of the six sectarian religious teachers. Thus I ask the Exalted One."

34. LET ME THEN SHAVE OFF MY HAIR AND BEARD

CY. He shows the thought behind the slave's eagerness to go forth to be as follows: "If I were to practice giving, in my whole life I would not be able to give even a hundredth part of what the king gives in a single day. [Therefore I will go forth.]"

CONTENT WITH THE SIMPLEST FOOD AND SHELTER

CY. Having abandoned improper ways of seeking (his food and shelter), he is content through the highest effacement.

SUB. CY. Or alternatively: established in a lofty state, his supreme and highest end is food and shelter; he does not seek or expect anything else of a material nature.

DELIGHTING IN SOLITUDE

CY. He delights in the three kinds of solitude stated thus: "There is bodily solitude (*kāyaviveka*) for those dwelling in physical solitude; there is mental solitude (*cittaviveka*) for those delighting in renunciation, for those who attain

33. See *The All-Embracing Net of Views*, pp. 173–78.

to the highest cleansing; and there is ultimate solitude (*upadhiviveka*) for those persons free from the acquisitions, for those who have gone beyond formations" (Nidd I 26). One person dwells alone in body, having abandoned the company of a group. One dwells alone by way of the eight meditative attainments, having abandoned the company of the mental defilements. And one dwells alone having attained *Nibbāna*, having entered the attainment of fruition or the attainment of cessation.

More Excellent Fruits

40. LISTEN, GREAT KING, AND ATTEND CAREFULLY

CY. Here, the word "listen" is an injunction to ward off distraction in the ear-faculty; the words "attend carefully" are an injunction to strengthen attention, to ward off distraction in the mind-faculty. The former is for preventing a distorted grasp of the phrasing, the latter for preventing a distorted grasp of the meaning. By the former he enjoins one to listen to the *Dhamma*, by the latter to retain in mind the *Dhamma* that has been heard, to examine it, etc. By the former he shows: "This *Dhamma* possesses phrasing (*sabyañjano*); therefore it should be heard." By the latter, he shows: "It possesses meaning (*sāttho*); therefore it should be carefully attended to." Or else the word "carefully" (*sādhukaṃ*) can be construed with both words ("listen" and "attend") thus: "Since this *Dhamma* is deep in doctrine and deep in teaching, listen carefully. Since it is deep in meaning and deep in penetration, attend to it carefully."

HEREIN, GREAT KING, A TATHĀGATA ARISES IN THE WORLD

CY. There are three kinds of world: the physical world, the world of sentient beings, and the world of formations; here the world of sentient beings is intended. When a *Tathāgata* arises in the world of beings, he does not arise in the world of the gods or in the Brahma-world but only in the human world. He does not arise in other world-systems within the human world but only in this one, and here too not everywhere but only in the middle region (northern India). Not only *Tathāgata*s, but *paccekabuddha*s, chief disciples, the eighty great elders, the mothers and fathers of Buddhas, world-ruling monarchs, and other prominent brahmins and householders arise only here.

From the time the *Tathāgata* was offered the meal of honey and milk-rice by Sujātā (on the eve of his Enlightenment) up to the time he reached the path of *arahatship*, he is said to have been "arising." With the attainment of the fruit of *arahatship*, he is said to have "arisen." Or alternatively, from the time of his great renunciation, or from the time (he descended from) the Tusita heaven, or from the time (he formed the aspiration for Buddhahood) at the feet of the Buddha Dīpaṅkara up to the time he reached the path of *arahatship*, he is said to have been "arising," and with the attainment of the fruit of *arahatship*, he is said to have "arisen." Here the word "arises" signifies the state of having arisen, explained in the first case. Thus the meaning is: "A *Tathāgata* has arisen in the world."

HAVING REALIZED BY HIS OWN DIRECT KNOWLEDGE

CY. By this phrase inferential knowledge, etc., are rejected.

SUB. CY. Inferential knowledge, analogy, implication of meaning, etc., are rejected, because the Exalted Buddhas have only one source of knowledge. For them everything is known by direct cognition, through the movement of their unimpeded faculty of knowledge.

THIS WORLD WITH ITS GODS, ETC.

CY. Therein, by the phrase "with its gods," the gods of the lower five sense-sphere heavens are included. By the phrase "(with) its Māras" the gods of the sixth sense-sphere heaven are included. By the phrase "(with) its Brahmās," the Brahmās such as those of Brahmā's retinue, etc., are included. The phrase "with its recluses and brahmins," includes both those recluses and brahmins who are hostile and opposed to the Buddha's dispensation, and those who have truly stilled and expelled evil.[34] The phrase "this generation" includes the world of sentient beings, and the phrase "with its rulers and people" includes conventional gods (i.e. rulers) and the rest of humanity.[35] Thus by the first three phrases here (qualifying "this world") the world of beings along with the physical world is included; by the word "generation" with its two qualifying phrases the world of beings only is included.

Another method: By mentioning "with its gods," the gods of the immaterial world are included; by mentioning "(with) its Māras," the gods of the six sense-sphere heavenly worlds are included; by mentioning "(with) its Brahmās," the gods of the fine-material Brahma-world are included; by mentioning "(this generation) with its recluses and brahmins," etc., the human world with its conventional gods (rulers) and its four social orders, or all the rest of the world of beings, is included.

Further, by the phrase "with its gods," the Buddha speaks of his realization of the entire world, delimiting it by the highest plane [for among the five destinations, the planes included in the destination of the gods are best; among these, the immaterial planes are very excellent due to their special qualities such as the removal of the suffering of the defilements, their endowment with peaceful, sublime, and imperturbable dwellings, and their extremely long life-span]. But some might think: "Māra is very powerful—he is the ruler and master of the six sense-sphere heavens. What, has the Buddha realized him, too?" Dispelling their doubts, he says: "(With) its Māras." Still others might think: "Brahmā is very powerful. With his ten fingers he radiates light over the ten-thousandfold world-systems, and he experiences the unsurpassed bliss of the jhānic attainments. What, has he

---

34. *Samitapāpa, bāhitapāpa:* the traditional textual etymologies of the words *samaṇa* and *brāhmaṇa,* respectively.

35. *Sadevamanussāya.* This phrase might have been rendered "with its gods and men," but I here follow the commentary in treating deva as "conventional gods", i.e., rulers, and *manussa* as the rest of humanity, exclusive of its rulers. In Pali *deva* is often used as a respectful address for a king.

realized him, too?" Dispelling their doubts, he says: "(With) its Brahmās." Then some think: "There are many recluses and brahmins opposed to the dispensation. What, has he realized them, too?" Dispelling their doubts, he says: "With its recluses and brahmins." Thus, having revealed his realization of the most excellent states, with the phrases "with its rulers and its people" he reveals his realization of the rest of the world of beings, delimiting it by way of its most excellent members with the reference to conventional gods (rulers) and the rest of humanity. Thus here is the sequence of terms stated by way of state [by way of the mental inclinations of others].

But the Ancients say that the phrase "with its gods" indicates the rest of the world together with the gods, "(with) its Māras" the rest of the world together with Māra, and "(with) its Brahmās" the rest of the world together with Brahmā. Thus with these three phrases he includes all beings found in the three planes of existence, presenting them under three different aspects, and with the next two phrases—"this generation with its recluses and brahmins, its rulers and people"—he again exhaustively treats the world. Thus, with these five phrases, the three realms of existence are exhaustively presented under different aspects.

He teaches the *Dhamma* that is good in the beginning, etc.

CY. Out of compassion for sentient beings, the Exalted One even leaves the unsurpassed happiness of solitude and teaches the *Dhamma*. And whether he teaches much or little, the *Dhamma* he teaches has the quality of being good in the beginning, etc. He teaches making it good, lovely, faultless, in the beginning, in the middle, and in the end.

An (individual) teaching (*desanā*) has a beginning, a middle, and an end, and the dispensation as a whole (*sāsana*) has a beginning, a middle, and an end. With regard to a teaching, even in a verse of four lines, the first line is the beginning, the two lines following it the middle, and the last line the end. In a *sutta* with a single sequence of meaning, the introduction is the beginning, the phrase "Thus spoke the Exalted One" is the end, and what comes in between these is the middle. In a *sutta* with several sequences of meaning, the first sequence is the beginning, the final sequence is the end, and what comes in between—whether one, two, or many—is the middle.

With regard to the dispensation, moral discipline, concentration, and insight are the beginning. For it is said: "What is the starting point of wholesome states? Well-purified moral discipline and straight view" (SN 47:3/S V 143). And since it is said, "There is, *bhikkhus*, a middle way awakened to by the *Tathāgata*" (SN 56:11/S V 421), the noble path is the middle. And the end is the fruit and *Nibbāna*. The fruit is called the end in the following passage: "This is the goal of the holy life, this is its essence, this is its end—(the unshakable liberation of the mind)" (MN 29/M I 197). And *Nibbāna* is called the end in this passage: "Friend Visākha, the holy life plunges into *Nibbāna*, *Nibbāna* is its final resort, *Nibbāna* is its end" (MN 44/M I 304).

Here, the beginning, middle, and end intended are those of the teaching. For when the Exalted One teaches the *Dhamma*, he teaches it showing moral discipline in the beginning, the path in the middle, and *Nibbāna* in the end. Thus it is said: "He teaches the *Dhamma* that is good in the beginning, good in the middle, and good in the end." Therefore, other preachers of the *Dhamma* also explain the *Dhamma* in this way.

Possessing meaning and phrasing (*sātthaṁ sabyañjanaṁ*)

CY. One whose teaching is concerned with explanations of food, men, women, etc., does not teach in a way "possessing meaning." But the Exalted One, having abandoned such kinds of teaching, presents a teaching concerned with the four foundations of mindfulness, etc. Therefore he teaches the *Dhamma* "possessing meaning."

One whose teaching lacks the complete variety of phrases, or who confuses the various kinds of sounds, is said to have a teaching that is "without phrasing." But the Exalted One teaches the *Dhamma* making it complete in phrasing, without slurring together any of the distinct kinds of sound. Therefore he teaches the *Dhamma* "possessing phrasing."

Fully complete and purified

CY. It is "fully complete" because there is nothing deficient in it and nothing excessive, nothing to add or to remove; it is "purified" because it is without corruption. In the case of one who teaches his doctrine with the intention of obtaining honor and gain, the teaching is impure. But the Exalted One teaches without regard for worldly ends, with a heart made gentle by the development of loving kindness, suffused with (the wish for) the welfare of others, with a mind established in delivering others [i.e. with a mind of compassionate intention fixed in the mode of lifting others up from all defilements and from the suffering of the round]. Therefore he teaches a purified *Dhamma*.

He reveals the holy life

CY. The word "holy life" (*brahmacariya*) is found (in the texts) with the following meanings: giving, service, the moral discipline of the five precepts, the four immeasurable states, abstinence from sexual intercourse, contentment with one's own marital partner, energy, the factors of the Uposatha observance, the noble path, and the entire dispensation.[36] Here it is used to mean the dispensation. Thus the passage under consideration should be understood as follows: "He teaches the *Dhamma* that is good in the beginning, etc., … fully complete and purified. And teaching it thus he reveals the holy life, the entire dispensation comprised in the threefold training (moral discipline, concentration, and wisdom)."

42. A householder, or a householder's son

CY. Why does he mention householders first? Because they are humble and because they are predominant. Generally, when those from noble families go forth they become conceited because of their birth. When those from brahmin families

---

36. The commentary here cites passages from the suttas illustrating these different meanings.

go forth they become conceited because of their knowledge of the mantras. When those from low-class families go forth they are not able to establish themselves well because of their low birth. But householders' boys, who plough the earth with sweat flowing from their armpits and backs glistening with perspiration, lack such conceit; thus they are humble and free from pride. When they go forth they do not become proud and conceited; rather, to the best of their ability, they learn the entire word of the Buddha, do the work of insight, and establish themselves in *arahatship*. And those who renounce and go forth from other families are not numerous, whereas those from householder families are. Thus, because they are humble and because they are predominant, householders are mentioned first.

THE HOUSEHOLD LIFE IS CROWDED, A PATH OF DUST

CY. Even if a couple, husband and wide, live in a house sixty cubits on an estate of a hundred yojanas, household life is still "crowded" in the sense that it involves obstacles [such as lust, etc.] and impediments [such as fields, land, etc.]. It is "a path of dust," that is, a path for the arising of the dust of lust, etc.

GOING FORTH IS LIKE THE OPEN AIR

CY. It is like the open air in the sense of being unhindered. For even if one gone forth is living in a gabled cottage, a jewel-ornamented mansion, or a celestial palace, etc., with closed doors and windows, covered by a roof, he is unhindered, unattached, unbound. Further, household life is crowded because it gives little opportunity for wholesome activity, and it is a path of dust because, like an unchecked dust-heap, it is a place where dust collects, i.e. the dust of the defilements. Going forth is like the open air in that it gives opportunity for wholesome activity as much as one pleases.

THE PERFECTLY COMPLETE, PERFECTLY PURIFIED HOLY LIFE

CY. The holy life of the threefold training is "perfectly

complete" because it is to be accomplished up to the last moment of consciousness, making it unbroken even for a single day. It is "perfectly purified" because it is to be accomplished up to the last moment of consciousness, making it untainted by the taint of defilements even for a single day.

44. HE COMES TO BE ENDOWED WITH WHOLESOME BODILY AND VERBAL ACTION, HIS LIVELIHOOD IS PURIFIED

CY. When "proper behavior and resort" are mentioned, wholesome bodily and verbal action are included. However, the moral discipline of purified livelihood does not arise in space or among the treetops, but in the doors of body and speech. Therefore, in order to show the doors where it arises, it is said: "He comes to be endowed with wholesome bodily and verbal action." And since he is endowed with that, his livelihood is purified.

On Moral Discipline

45–62. (For explanations of the training rules observed by the *bhikkhu*, the commentator refers to the exegesis of the sections on moral discipline included in the commentary to the *Brahmajāla Sutta*. Some of these remarks have been incorporated into the English renderings themselves. For further amplification, see *The All-Embracing Net of Views*, pp. 118–25.)

63. (HE) SEES NO DANGER ANYWHERE

CY. He does not see any danger anywhere from the dangers which might arise rooted in nonrestraint. Why? Because, due to his restraint, he does not face any danger rooted in nonrestraint.

HE EXPERIENCES WITHIN HIMSELF A BLAMELESS HAPPINESS (*ANAVAJJA-SUKHA*)

CY. He experiences within himself a blameless, faultless, wholesome bodily and mental happiness accompanied by such phenomena as non-remorse, gladness, rapture, and tranquillity, which are based on moral discipline as their proximate cause.

Restraint of Sense Faculties (*Indriyasaṃvara*)

64. HAVING SEEN A FORM WITH THE EYE

CY. The word "eye" (*cakkhu*) is found in the texts with the following meanings:

(i) the Buddha eye, as it is said: "he surveyed the world with the eye of a Buddha" (MN 26/M I 169);
(ii) the universal eye, the knowledge of omniscience, as it is said: "Ascend the palace of *Dhamma*, O greatly wise one, O universal eye!" (MN 26/M I 168);
(iii) the eye of *Dhamma*, the wisdom of the lower three paths, as it is said: "There arose in him the dust-free, stainless eye of *Dhamma*" (MN 74/M I 501);
(iv) the wisdom eye, the knowledge of past lives [and the knowledge of the destruction of the cankers], as it is said: "The eye arose, knowledge arose" (Vin I 11);
(v) the divine eye (as in the *Sāmaññaphala Sutta*, §97);
(vi) the eye as a sense organ, as it is said: "In dependence on the eye and forms eye-consciousness arises" (MN 18/M I 111).

Here the word "eye," which conventionally signifies the eye as a sense organ, is used to signify eye-consciousness. Therefore the meaning of the above statement is: "Having seen a form with eye-consciousness." Everything else that needs to be said concerning the other terms has been said already in the *Visuddhimagga* (I.53–59, pp. 20–24).

HE EXPERIENCES WITHIN HIMSELF AN UNBLEMISHED HAPPINESS (*ABYĀSEKA-SUKHA*)

CY. He experiences the purified happiness of the higher

consciousness (*adhicitta-sukha*), which is unblemished, unadulterated since it is devoid of the blemish of defilements.

SUB. CY. "The happiness of the higher consciousness": this is said because, when restraint of the sense faculties is fully purified, the principal evil phenomena [the hindrances] disappear and as a result devotion to the higher consciousness is easily obtained.

Mindfulness and Clear Comprehension (*Sati-sampajañña*) [37]

1. On Going Forward and Returning

65. ON GOING FORWARD AND RETURNING

CY. Here, "going forward" is going, "returning" is turning back. Both of these are found in all four postures. First, in going (walking), "going forward" is bringing the body forward, "returning" is turning around. In standing, when one who is standing bends the body forward, that is "going forward"; when he draws the body back, that is "returning." In sitting, when one who is sitting shifts forward towards the front portion of the seat, that is "going forward"; when he shifts backwards towards the back portion of the seat, that is "returning." The same method of explanation applies to lying down [that is, by way of the shifting forward and backward of the one lying down].

THE *BHIKKHU* ACTS WITH CLEAR COMPREHENSION (*SAMPAJĀNAKĀRĪ HOTI*).

CY. He does all his tasks with clear comprehension. Or he

---

37. An earlier translation of the entire section on mindfulness and clear comprehension, drawn from the commentaries to the *Satipaṭṭhāna Sutta*, is included in Soma Thera, *The Way of Mindfulness*, pp. 60-100.

practices clear comprehension itself. For he practices clear comprehension when engaged in going forward, etc.; he is never lacking in clear comprehension.

SUB. CY. One clearly comprehending (*sampajāno*) is one who knows comprehensively [in various ways] or eminently, in a distinguished way. The state of one clearly comprehending is clear comprehension (*sampajañña*), that is, it is the knowledge occurring in the way just described.

N. SUB. CY. The teacher Ānanda Thera (author of the *Abhidhamma* subcommentary) says: "Clearly comprehending is understanding comprehensively, rightly, and evenly (*samantato, sammā, samaṃ vā pajānanaṃ sampajānaṃ*). That itself is clear comprehension."

One who "acts with clear comprehension" is one who habitually does all his tasks with clear comprehension or one who habitually practices clear comprehension. Another method of explanation distinct from that of the commentary is this: as it arouses non-delusion in regard to (all such actions as) going forward, etc., it is the practice of clear comprehension. One in whom there is this practice of clear comprehension is one who "acts with clear comprehension."

CY. Clear comprehension is fourfold: clear comprehension of purposefulness, clear comprehension of suitability, clear comprehension of the resort, and clear comprehension of non-delusion.[38]

SUB. CY. What is purposeful is what accords with the purpose, that is, with growth in the *Dhamma*. Clear comprehension of purposefulness is clearly comprehending what is purposeful in (such activities) as going forward, etc. Clear comprehension of suitability is clearly comprehending what is suitable, beneficial, for oneself. Clear comprehension of the resort is clearly comprehending the resort for one's almsround, and also clearly comprehending the resort of one's meditation subject, not abandoning it when engaged in other activities such

38. In Pali: *sātthaka-sampajañña, sappāya-sampajañña, gocara-sampajañña, asammoha-sampajañña.*

as going forward, etc. Clear comprehension of non-delusion is the clear comprehension which does not become deluded about (such activities) as going forward, etc.

CY. (i) Therein, *clear comprehension of purposefulness* is the discernment of a worthwhile purpose (in going forward) after examining the action to determine whether or not it has a worthwhile purpose. Thus, when the thought of going forward has arisen, one does not go at once following the impulse of the mind, but considers: "Is there some worthwhile purpose in my going there or not?" The purpose aimed at here, growth in the *Dhamma*, can be served by going to see a *cetiya*,[39] a Bodhi tree, the *Saṅgha*, elder *bhikkhus*, an unattractive object (i.e. a corpse that can serve as a meditation subject), etc. For by seeing a *cetiya* or a Bodhi tree one arouses rapture having the Buddha as object, and by seeing the *Saṅgha* one arouses rapture having the *Saṅgha* as object. Exploring that rapture by way of its destruction and falling away, one attains *arahatship*. By seeing elder *bhikkhus* one can be established in their exhortation, and by seeing an unattractive object one can arouse the first *Jhāna*. Exploring that *Jhāna* by way of its destruction and falling away, one attains *arahatship*. Therefore to go and see these is purposeful.

SUB. CY. "One attains *arahatship*": this exposition mentions the highest aim. But even the arousing of serenity and insight is growth for a *bhikkhu*.

CY. Some [the residents of the Abhayagiri Vihāra] say that the gaining of material requisites is also a worthwhile purpose, since it is undertaken to assist the holy life, which depends upon them.

(ii) *Clear comprehension of suitability* is the discernment of suitability in the act of going after examining it to determine whether it is suitable or unsuitable. For example, going to see a *cetiya* is purposeful. But when a great devotional offering is

---

39. *Cetiya*, also called a *thūpa* (Skt. *stūpa*): a dome-shaped memorial shrine often holding sacred objects, such as relics of the Buddha or eminent monks.

being made to the *cetiya*, a large crowd of people covering an area of ten or twelve yojanas assembles, and men and women wander around, decked in ornaments appropriate to their status, looking like painted dolls. In this situation greed can arise towards a desirable object, aversion towards an undesirable object, and delusion can arise through indifference. One may commit the disciplinary offence of bodily contact[40] or may meet some obstacle to one's life or to the holy life. In such a case that place is unsuitable. But if there are no such obstacles it is suitable. The same explanation applies in the case of going to see a Bodhi tree.

Going to see the *Saṅgha* is purposeful. But when people build a great pavilion in the village and arrange for an all-night preaching of the *Dhamma*, a crowd assembles and the aforesaid obstacles arise. In such a case that place is unsuitable. But if there are no such obstacles, it is suitable. The same explanation applies in the case of going to see elder *bhikkhus* surrounded by a large retinue.

Going to see an unattractive object (i.e. a corpse) is purposeful. To illustrate this, the following story is told: One young *bhikkhu*, it is said, took a novice and went to get wood for making toothpicks. The novice stepped down from the road and, walking a little way, saw a corpse. (Using the corpse as a meditation object), he developed the first *Jhāna*. He made that *Jhāna* his basis for insight, explored its formations, realized three fruits (up to the fruit of non-returner) and stood discerning the meditation subject with the aim of attaining the next path (the path of *arahatship*). Meanwhile the young *bhikkhu*, not seeing the novice, called out to him. The novice thought: "From the day I went forth I have never made a *bhikkhu* call me twice. I will attain the next stage of distinction some other day." Then he replied: "What is it, venerable sir?" "Come," said the *bhikkhu*. The novice came as soon as he was called and told the *bhikkhu*: "Venerable sir, go along this path a little way. Then stand in the same place where I stood facing east and look about in front of you for a few moments." The *bhikkhu* did so and reached the

---

40. The second *saṅghādisesa* offence, touching a woman with a lustful mind.

same attainments of distinction. Thus one unattractive object served the purpose of two people.

Though (going to see) a corpse is purposeful, the corpse of a woman is not suitable for a man, and the corpse of a man is not suitable for a woman. Only a corpse of a member of the same sex is suitable.

Thus clear comprehension of suitability is the discernment of suitability.

(iii) *Clear comprehension of the resort.* The resort (*gocara*) is the meditation subject agreeable to oneself, selected from among the thirty-eight meditation subjects. When one who has discerned purposefulness and suitability, and learned the resort of his meditation subject, goes along the resort of his almsround keeping in mind that meditation subject, that is clear comprehension of the resort.[41] In order to explicate this, the following tetrad should be understood: Herein, (1) one *bhikkhu* takes it but does not bring it back; (2) one does not take it but brings it back; (3) one neither takes it nor brings it back; and (4) one both takes it and brings it back.

SUB. CY. "One takes it": one practices the meditation subject, devotes himself to it, until he starts to return from his almsround. "But does not take it back": he does not bring back the meditation subject from the time he takes his meal until he arrives back at his day-quarters.

CY. (1) "One who takes it but does not bring it back": Among these, one *bhikkhu* cleanses his mind of obstructive states by walking and sitting in meditation during the day and in the first watch of the night. In the middle watch of the night he sleeps, and in the last watch he again sits and walks. Early in the morning he does the duties connected with the terraces around the *cetiya* and the Bodhi tree, waters the Bodhi tree, fills the vessels for drinking water and washing water, and does all the various duties towards his preceptor and teacher, etc., as prescribed in the Khandhakas. Then, after seeing to the needs of the body [washing the face, etc.],

41. The word *gocara*, "resort," has two meanings combined in the above definition: the meditation subject and the alms resort.

he enters his dwelling place and warms up (his practice) for two or three sittings, devoting himself to his meditation subject. At the time for the almsround he rises and keeping in mind his meditation subject, he takes his robe and bowl, leaves his dwelling place, and goes to the terrace of the *cetiya*, still attending to the meditation subject. If his meditation subject is the recollection of the Buddha, he enters the terrace of the *cetiya* without relinquishing it. But if it is some other subject, then, while standing at the foot of the steps (leading to the terrace), he should put it aside as if it were a bundle held in the hand and joyfully take up the Buddha as the object of meditation. Having climbed up to the terrace, he should circumambulate the *cetiya* three times, venerating it at four points if it is a large *cetiya* and at eight points if it is a small one.

After venerating the *cetiya*, the *bhikkhu* should go to the terrace of the Bodhi tree and venerate the Bodhi tree, displaying a humble manner just as if he were in the presence of the Exalted Buddha himself. Having thus venerated both the *cetiya* and the Bodhi tree, he returns to the place where he deposited his meditation subject (i.e. the foot of the steps) and again takes up the original meditation subject as if picking up his bundle with his hand. Keeping his meditation subject in mind, he robes himself just outside the village and enters the village for alms.

Then the people, seeing him, exclaim: "Our venerable has come," and they go to meet him, take his bowl, offer him a seat in their house or sitting hall, and give him congee. While the food is being prepared they wash his feet, anoint them with oil, and sitting in front of him ask questions or express their wish to hear the *Dhamma*. The teachers of the commentaries say that even if they do not ask him to speak, he should still give the people a talk on *Dhamma* in order to help them; for there is no talk on *Dhamma* disconnected from meditation. Therefore, he gives them a talk on *Dhamma*, eats his meal, and expresses thanks, all the while keeping his meditation subject in mind. Then he departs, accompanied by the people, who follow him despite his efforts to turn them back. Having left the village, he turns the people back and takes the road back to his monastery.

When the novices and younger *bhikkhus*, who had finished their meal outside the village and returned to the monastery before him, see the *bhikkhu* coming, they go out to meet him and take his bowl and robes. In olden times, it is said that the *bhikkhus* performed their duties towards their elders without even looking at their face to see if the elder was their preceptor or teacher; they did their duties as soon as the elder arrived.

Then the novices and younger *bhikkhus* ask him: "Venerable sir, who are those people? Are they your maternal or paternal relatives?"

"What makes you ask?" he asks.

"They showed you such affection and esteem."

"Friends, even our parents would find it difficult to help us in the way these people do. Our very bowls and robes belong to them. Because of their support, we do not know fear in time of fear and do not know famine in time of famine. There is no one so helpful to us as these people." Thus he goes on speaking about their virtues. This is called "a *bhikkhu* who takes it but does not bring it back."

(2) "One who does not take it but brings it back": Another *bhikkhu* performs the aforesaid duties early in the morning. While he is doing so, the *kamma*-born heat element blazes up and burns his stomach. Sweat pours forth from his body and he cannot keep track of his meditation subject [since one whose body is afflicted with hunger cannot concentrate well]. While it is still early, he takes his bowl and robe, hastily venerates the *cetiya*, and enters the village for congee and almsfood while the cattle are still leaving their pens for the pasture. Receiving some congee, he goes to the sitting hall and drinks it. As soon as he has swallowed two or three mouthfuls, the *kamma*-born heat element lets go of the stomach and grasps the ingested food. Like a man who has bathed with a hundred buckets of water, the burning of the heat element is extinguished. He drinks the rest of the congee with his mind on his meditation subject, washes his bowl and cleans his mouth, and spends the period between meals attending to his meditation subject. Afterwards he walks for alms in the remaining places and takes his meal keeping his

meditation subject in mind. Following the meal he returns to the monastery taking his meditation subject, which he attends to without interruption. This is called "one who does not take it but brings it back." And such *bhikkhus* in the Buddha's dispensation who have aroused insight and attained *arahatship* after drinking congee cannot be counted. In the island of Sri Lanka alone, in the sitting halls of various villages there is not even a single seat where a *bhikkhu* did not attain *arahatship* after drinking congee.

(3) "One who neither takes it nor brings it back": The third *bhikkhu* lives negligently. He neglects the task, violates all the duties, and dwells with a mind hindered by the five mental stumbling blocks and the five mental bonds. He enters the village for alms without even entertaining the idea that there is such a thing as a meditation subject. While walking for alms and eating his meal he associates with householders in improper ways and he leaves empty. This is called "a *bhikkhu* who neither takes it nor brings it back."

N. SUB. CY. "He neglects the task': he does not arouse energy, does not take up the task of devotion to meditative development. "He violates all the duties" by not fulfilling the practice of the duties. The five mental stumbling blocks (*cetokhīlā*) and the five mental bonds (*cetaso vinibandhā*) are explained in the *Majjhima Nikāya*, in the Discourse on the Mental Stumbling Blocks (*Cetokhila Sutta*, MN 16):

"*Bhikkhus*, what are the five mental stumbling blocks that are not abandoned? Herein, a *bhikkhu* has doubts about the Teacher, doubts about the *Dhamma*, doubts about the *Saṅgha*, doubts about the training, and he is angry with his companions in the holy life.

"And what are the five mental bonds that are not cut off? Herein, a *bhikkhu* is not devoid of lust for sense pleasures, not devoid of lust for the body, not devoid of lust for material form; after filling his stomach, he lives devoted to the pleasures of sleeping, relaxing, and dozing; and he lives the holy life aspiring to rebirth in some order of gods" (M I 101–102).

The former set (the stumbling blocks) consists of doubt and hatred, the latter set (the mental bonds) consists of greed. He "leaves empty" because he is devoid of a meditation subject.

CY. (4) "One who both takes it and brings it back": This *bhikkhu* should be understood by way of the duty of going and returning (*gatapaccāgatavatta*). For sons of good family, desiring their own welfare, go forth from home to homelessness in the Buddha's dispensation. When they dwell together in a group of ten, twenty, thirty, forty, fifty or a hundred, they make a pact among themselves thus: "Friends, you have not gone forth because you were oppressed by debts, or because you were oppressed by fear, or because you were concerned for the material requisites of life. You went forth because you desired liberation from suffering. Therefore, whenever a defilement arises while you are going (walking), you should restrain it while you are still going; likewise if a defilement arises while you are standing, you should restrain it while you are still standing; if while sitting, restrain it while sitting, and if while lying down, restrain it while lying down."

(Along the road to the alms resort) there are stones placed at intervals of a half-*usabha*, *usabha*, half-*gāvuta*, and *gāvuta*.[42] After making that pact, whenever the *bhikkhus* would go on almsround they would walk along attending to their meditation subject [noting the place they had reached] by their perception of the stones. If any *bhikkhu* gave rise to a defilement while going, he would restrain it while still going. If he could not do so he would stand still; the *bhikkhu* coming along behind him would also stand still. [The former stood still because he did not want to raise his foot with a mind dissociated from his meditation subject, the latter because he did not want to bypass the one standing in front of him.] The former *bhikkhu* would then admonish himself: "The *bhikkhu* behind you knows that a defiled thought has arisen in you; that thought is unsuitable for you." Having thus admonished himself, he develops insight and right on the spot enters the plane of the noble ones. But if he still could not do so he would sit down. Then the *bhikkhu* coming along behind him would also sit down, and so on, as before. Even if the *bhikkhu*

---

42. Ancient Indian measurements. An *usabha* is about twenty yards, a *gāvuta* eighty *usabhas*.

could not enter the plane of the noble ones, he would suppress the defilements and continue on his way attending to the meditation subject. But he would not raise his foot with a mind dissociated from his meditation subject. If he should do so he would turn around and go back [to the place where he took his first step with a mind dissociated from his meditation subject].

An example of this practice is the Elder Mahāphussadeva, the verandah-dweller. It is said that he spent nineteen years fulfilling the duty of going and returning. People at work—ploughing, sowing, threshing, and doing other jobs—would see the Elder coming along the road in such a manner and say to each other: "The Elder turns back again and again. Has he lost his way? Or has he forgotten something?" But he remained unconcerned, and doing the work of a recluse with a mind devoted to his meditation subject, in the middle of his twentieth rains residence he attained *arahatship*. On the day of his attainment a deity living at the end of his walkway stood emitting light from his fingers. The Four Great Kings of the gods, Sakka the lord of the gods, and Brahmā Sahampati came to serve him. The Elder Mahātissa the forest dweller saw the radiance and the next day asked the Elder: "During the night there was a radiance surrounding the venerable one. What was that?" The Elder Mahāphussa tried to divert the talk by saying: "Radiance? There is the radiance of a lamp, the radiance of gems," and so forth. But the other pressed him saying: "You are concealing yourself." Finally he admitted this and reported his attainment.

Another example is the Elder Mahānāga, who dwelt at the Black Creeper Pavilion. It is said that while fulfilling the observance of going and returning he first made the determination to adhere only to the postures of standing and walking for seven years, thinking: "I will honor the great exertion of the Exalted One." After fulfilling the observance of going and returning for another sixteen years, he attained *arahatship*.

SUB. CY. "Only to the postures of standing and walking": This is said by way of the postures determined upon, not as a refusal to sit down when taking food, etc., as it is then necessary to sit. With the word "only" he refuses to lie down or to sit down on other occasions (when it is not necessary to sit). The "great exertion of the Exalted One" was his practice of austerities. He thought: "For our sakes the Protector of the World practiced austerities for six years. I will honor him as best I can." For to honor the Teacher by practice is the more praiseworthy way of honoring him. Not so praiseworthy is the honoring of him with material offerings.

CY. He walked along raising his feet with his mind devoted to his meditation subject. If he raised his feet with a mind dissociated from the subject, he turned around and went back. Having come to the vicinity of the village, he would stand in an area (at such a distance from the village) that people would wonder whether he was a cow or a monk, and there would robe himself. Then, after washing his almsbowl with water from his water bottle, he would fill his mouth with water. For what reason? He thought: "When people come to give me alms or to venerate me, let me not be distracted from my meditation subject even by merely saying 'May you live long' to them." But if people asked about the date, or the number of *bhikkhus*, or some other question, he would swallow the water and answer. If no one questioned him about the day, etc., at the time of leaving he would spit the water out near the village gate and continue on his way.

Another example is the fifty *bhikkhus* who spent the rains residence at the monastery of Kalambatittha. On the full-moon day of July[43] they made the pact: "As long as we have not attained *arahatship* we will not converse with one another." When they entered the village for alms, they did so after filling their mouths with water. When asked about the date, etc., they acted in the way explained in the previous case. When people saw the spots where they spit out the water (after leaving the village), they would know: "One came today, two came," etc. They thought: "Is it only us with whom these monks do not speak or also with one another? If they do not speak to one another there must be some dispute between them. Let us go and make them pardon

43. The beginning of the rains residence.

each other." Having gone to the monastery, they did not see even two of the fifty *bhikkhus* in one place. Then one perceptive man in the group said: "The dwelling place of people who are quarrelling does not look like this. The terraces of the *cetiya* and the Bodhi tree are neatly swept, the brooms are neatly put away, drinking water and washing water are neatly set up." Thereupon they returned. Within the three months (of the rains residence) those *bhikkhus* attained *arahatship* and at the great *pavāraṇā* held their *pavāraṇā* ceremony in purity.[44]

Thus the *bhikkhu* who "both takes it and brings it back" is one like the Elder Mahānāga who dwelt at the Black Creeper Pavilion and the *bhikkhus* who spent the rains residence at the monastery of Kalambatittha. He walks along raising his feet with a mind entirely devoted to his meditation subject. Having gone to the vicinity of the village, he fills his mouth with water, examines the streets, and only enters a street where there are no quarrelsome drunkards, or derelicts, etc.; and no wild elephants or horses, etc. Walking for alms there, he does not go quickly as if in a hurry. For the ascetic practice of going on almsround is not to be undertaken quickly. He goes, rather, slowly and leisurely like a water cart that has reached uneven ground.

When he has entered among the houses, he examines whether or not the people in the houses he approaches wish to give alms, waiting in front of the house for an appropriate length of time. When he obtains almsfood, he takes it and either goes to some place inside or outside the village or returns to the monastery itself. There, attending to his meditation subject, he sits down in a suitable comfortable place and establishes the perception of the repulsiveness in nutriment, reflecting upon the food by way of the similes of greasing an axle, applying ointment to a wound, and eating one's own son's flesh. Then he eats the food, aware of the eight factors in the use of food, thus: "I make use of this almsfood not for amusement, nor for intoxication, nor for adornment, nor for beautification. I use it only for the support and

44. The *pavāraṇā* is the ceremony held at the conclusion of the residence.

maintenance of this body, for preventing harm, and for assisting the holy life." After finishing his meal, he washes up and takes a short rest to dispel the fatigue caused by the meal. Then in the afternoon, the first watch of the night, and the last watch he attends to his meditation subject, just as in the forenoon.

By fulfilling the observance of going and returning, "taking" the meditation subject in mind when setting out on the almsround and "bringing it back" when returning, if one has sufficient supporting conditions one attains *arahatship* in the first stage of life; if one does not attain it in the first stage of life, then in the middle stage; if not in the middle stage, then at the time of death. If one does not attain it at the time of death, then one attains it (in one's next life) as a young god. If one does not attain *arahatship* as a young god, then, if born at a time when a Buddha has not arisen in the world, one realizes the enlightenment of a *paccekabuddha*. If one does not realize the enlightenment of a *paccekabuddha*, then one attains *arahatship* in the presence of a Buddha—as one with quick understanding like the Elder Bāhiya Ḍārucīriya, or as one with great wisdom like the Elder Sāriputta, or as one with great supernormal power like the Elder Mahāmoggallāna, or as an exponent of the ascetic practices like the Elder Mahākassapa, or as one with the divine eye like the Elder Anuruddha, or as a master of the *Vinaya* like the Elder Upāli, or as an expounder of the *Dhamma* like the Elder Puṇṇa Mantāniputta, or as a forest-dweller like the Elder Revata, or as one highly learned like the Elder Ānanda, or as one desiring the training like the Elder Rāhula. Thus in the tetrad of "taking and bringing back" the *bhikkhu* who both takes (the meditation subject on his almsround) and brings it back is the one who attains the peak in the clear comprehension of the resort.

(iv) *Clear comprehension of non-delusion* is the clear comprehension which does not become deluded about going forward, etc. It should be understood as follows.

Herein, when going forward and returning, a *bhikkhu* does not become deluded about these actions like the blind and foolish worldling who deludedly thinks: "A self goes forward, the action of going forward is produced by a self," or "I go forward, the action of going forward is produced by me." Instead he undeludedly understands: When the thought "Let me go forward" arises, the mind-originated air element arises together with that thought, producing [bodily] intimation.[45] Thus through the diffusion of the air element (originating from) mental activity, this set of bones conceived of as the body goes forward. When going forward, in each act of raising the foot two elements—the earth element and the water element—are subordinate and weak, while the other two elements [the air element and the heat element] are predominant and strong. So too in bringing the foot forward and in shifting it away. But in dropping the foot two elements—the heat element and the air element—are subordinate and weak, while the other two elements [the earth element and the water element] are predominant and strong. So too in placing the foot on the ground and in pressing the foot against the ground.

SUB. CY. By the phrase "A self goes forward," he shows how the blind worldling becomes deluded about the activity of going forward due to the obsession of views; by the phrase "I go forward," he shows delusion due to the obsession of conceit. Since neither of these (views and conceit) occurs without craving, delusion due to the obsession of craving is also (implicitly) shown. "Instead he undeludedly understands": he shows how there is non-delusion through the dissection of the compact (*ghanavinibbhoga*).

---

45. The air element, in early Buddhist physiology, is the physical factor responsible for bodily movement. The mind initiates and regulates the movements of the body by originating a particular type of air element which in turn produces bodily intimation (*kāya-viññatti*). Bodily intimation is defined in the commentaries as "the mode (conformation) and the alteration (deformation) in the consciousness originated air element that causes the occurrence of moving forward, etc., which mode and alteration are a condition for the stiffening, upholding, and moving of the conascent material body" (*Vism* XIV, 61). According to the *Abhidhamma*, bodily intimation and verbal intimation endure only for a single thought-moment, unlike other material phenomena which have a duration of seventeen thought-moments.

"In each act of raising the foot," etc.: the heat element is the primary principle of motion in the act of raising the foot and the air element is its assistant. Since the heat element assisted by the air element is thus the condition for raising the foot, these two elements, through their efficacy, are predominant here; the other two are subordinate [because they lack that efficacy].

"So too in bringing the foot forward and in shifting it away": the air element is the primary principle of motion in the horizontal movement of the foot, and thus its function is prominent in the acts of bringing the foot forward and shifting it away; the heat element is its assistant. Since the air element assisted by the heat element is thus the condition for bringing the foot forward and shifting it away, these two elements, through their efficacy, are predominant here; the other two are subordinate [because they lack that efficacy].

Even though (in these two cases) the heat element and the air element are differently distinguished as assistant (*anugamaka*) and assisted (*anugantabba*), referring to their mere presence the commentator groups them together and says "so too."

"Raising the foot": lifting a foot from the place upon which it is treading.

"Bringing it forward": taking the foot past the place where one has been standing and bringing it in front.

"Shifting it away": taking the foot to the side to avoid a tree stump, etc., or to avoid contact with the foot placed on the ground.

Or alternatively, the distinction between these two terms can be understood thus: "bringing the foot forward" means bringing it as far as the foot placed on the ground, "shifting it away" means taking it beyond that point.

"But in dropping the foot": the water element is naturally heavier, and in dropping the foot the earth element is its assistant. Since the water element assisted by the earth element is the condition for dropping the foot, these two elements, through their efficacy, are predominant here; the other two are subordinate [because they lack that efficacy].

"So too in placing the foot on the ground and in pressing the foot against the ground": this is said because the earth element assisted by the water element is the condition for placing the foot on the ground. In keeping the foot on the ground, too, as if it were fixed, the water element is the assistant of the earth element, due to prominence of the latter's function. Similarly, the pressing of the foot against the ground is accomplished by way of the earth element through its activity of making contact; and in this case, too, the water element is the assistant of the earth element.

CY. Therein, when raising the foot, the material and mental phenomena which then occur do not reach the stage of bringing the foot forward. Similarly, those which occur when bringing the foot forward do not reach the stage of shifting it away; those which occur when shifting the foot away do not reach the stage of dropping it; those which occur when dropping the foot do not reach the stage of placing it on the ground; and those which occur when placing the foot on the ground do not reach the stage of pressing it against the ground.

Having come into being section by section, phase by phase, stage by stage, these phenomena break up right on the spot, popping like sesame seeds thrown onto a hot pan. Therein, who is the one that goes forward? To whom does the going forward pertain? For ultimately there is only the going of elements, the standing of elements, the sitting of elements, the lying down of elements. In each portion, together with the material form:

> One state of consciousness arises,
> Another state of consciousness ceases;
> The process thus goes on
> In uninterrupted flow like a stream.

Thus clear comprehension of non-delusion means not becoming deluded about (such actions as) going forward, etc. This concludes (the explanation of) the meaning of the phrase: "in going forward and returning, the *bhikkhu* acts with clear comprehension."

SUB. CY. "Therein": in the action of going forward, or in each of its portions mentioned above, such as raising the foot, etc. "When raising the foot": at the moment of raising the foot. "The material and mental phenomena": the material phenomena which occur in the mode of raising the foot, and the mental phenomena which originate that action. "Do not reach the stage of bringing the foot forward": because they last merely for a moment.

"Having come into being section by section," etc.: all this, it should be understood, is said with reference to (those phenomena) in each portion of the act of raising the foot, etc., by way of their belonging to a common continuity.

"These phenomena break up right on the spot": wherever they have arisen, just there (they break up). For phenomena do not move from one region to another [because of their rapid change].[46] The moment during which even material phenomena occur is extremely brief, more fleeting even than the encounter of the young gods fond of travel who wear sharp-edged razors bound to their heads and feet and run in opposite directions, upwards and downwards.[47]

"Popping like sesame seeds": this is said to show that just as the breakup of sesame seeds is characterized by the popping sound they make when they break up, so too for the arising of conditioned phenomena.

N. SUB. CY. Conditioned phenomena, of course, do not actually make a popping sound when they arise; this is said with an analogical meaning. For just as the popping sound is the characteristic indicating the breakup of sesame seeds, so arising is the characteristic indicating the breakup

---

46. Since phenomena, according to the Abhidhammic conception of *dhamma*s, are only of momentary duration, at the basic ontological level motion signifies, not the actual movement of an enduring entity from one place to another, but the successive arisings in adjacent locations (*desantar'uppatti*) of different phenomena belonging to the same continuum of events.

47. Perhaps this is a reference to certain astronomical phenomena (comets, shooting stars, etc.) conceived of as the activity of the devas.

of conditioned phenomena, since once they have arisen they invariably break up.

"Who is the one that goes forward?" There is no one who goes forward. Can it be said "To whom does the going forward pertain?" No, it cannot. Why? "For ultimately there is only the going of elements," etc.: this statement rejects the going forward of the self (accepted by) the blind deluded worldling, or, alternatively, the questions are posed by way of criticism, and the answer, "For ultimately," etc., is stated as the way of clearing the criticism.

"In each portion": in each of the six previously stated portions of the act of walking. The phrase "together with the material form" should be connected with the lines in the stanza (ending with the words) "arises" and "ceases." In connection with the first line, the material form is any material form arising simultaneously (with a state of consciousness). In connection with the second line, "the material form" refers to that same material form, having a duration of seventeen mind-moments, which had been already arisen (and existing) at the arising moment of the seventeenth state of consciousness subsequent to the ceasing of that state of consciousness with which it arose, and which ceases together with the cessation of that (seventeenth) state of consciousness. Otherwise, material and mental phenomena might be considered to have the same duration, and if this were so, one would be contradicted by such commentarial statements as "Material form changes sluggishly and ceases slowly" (Vibh-a 24) and by such canonical statements as "*Bhikkhus*, I do not see any other thing that changes so rapidly as the mind" (AN 1:49/A I 10). For it is the intrinsic nature of mind and mental factors to take an object, and they arise making manifest, according to their ability, that thing which serves as their object condition. Therefore their cessation takes place immediately after they have actualized their intrinsic nature (of cognizing the object). But material phenomena do not take an object; they are to be revealed by cognition. Thus the actualization of their being, to be revealed by cognition, lasts for sixteen states of consciousness. Therefore the duration of material phenomena is held to be equal to seventeen mind-moments (the sixteen just mentioned) together with the one mind-moment of the past (when the material phenomenon has arisen but the cognition of it has not yet begun).[48]

Consciousness changes so rapidly because it occurs through such conditions as the mere coming together of the three mental aggregates (feeling, perception, and mental formations) with an especially rapidly changing consciousness, and through the mere coming together of that consciousness with its objective domain. Material form is sluggish to change because its conditions are the ponderous primary elements. But the knowledge of the diversity of elements as they really are belongs to the *Tathāgata* alone, and by means of that knowledge he has stated that only material phenomena serve as pre-nascence condition, and by the same (faculty of knowledge) he has described the post-nascence condition.[49] Thus it is not tenable to maintain that material and mental phenomena have the same duration. Therefore the meaning here should be understood in the way stated. The point has been stated in this way because it is easy to understand the simultaneous cessation (of a state of mind and) the act of intimation accompanying that state of mind.

Hence the meaning (of the verse) should be understood thus: "Another state of consciousness ceases together with the material form which had arisen at the arising moment of the

---

48. This stipulation of seventeen mind-moments as the duration of one unit of material form is based on the *Abhidhamma* teaching that a complete cognitive process directed to an external sense object consists of seventeen states of consciousness: three in which the object merely impinges on the life continuum, and fourteen in which the actual cognition occurs. This process will be discussed more fully below.

49. According to the *Paṭṭhāna* system of conditional relations, the previously arisen object and sense faculty serve as pre-nascent conditions for the states of mind and mental factors that arise through their impingement, while states of mind and mental factors serve as post-nascent condition for the pre-existent material body.

seventeenth state of consciousness preceding it, and which existed along with the act of intimation." The first couplet of the verse should actually be construed thus:

> One state of consciousness ceases,
> Another state of consciousness arises.

For the sequence of meaning is different from the sequence of the words. For when the previously arisen state of consciousness ceases, in ceasing it becomes a proximity condition etc., for another state of consciousness arising immediately after itself.[50] Thus "another state of consciousness arises" possessing (that preceding state of consciousness as) its condition. And the difference here follows from the distinction in their stages.

If so, the criticism might be made that an interval can be found between the two (states of consciousness). To remove that criticism, he says: "In uninterrupted flow." Thus the mental continuum and the material continuum occur "like a stream," that is, like the current of water in a river.

---

50. Proximity condition (*anantarapaccaya*) is the relationship of a preceding moment of consciousness to its immediate successor in the same continuum of consciousness; the "etc." is intended to include other conditions that are applicable, such as contiguity condition (*samanantarapaccaya*). N.Sub.Cy's argument, briefly put, is that the verse must be construed to be saying, not that a single act of consciousness arises and ceases simultaneously with a unit of matter, but that while one unit of matter endures seventeen states of consciousness arise and cease.

2. On Looking Ahead and Aside

ON LOOKING AHEAD AND LOOKING ASIDE HE ACTS WITH CLEAR COMPREHENSION

CY. Here, "looking ahead" is looking in front, "looking aside" is looking in the side directions. The other kinds of looking—looking downwards, looking upwards, and looking back—are not mentioned here. Only these two are mentioned by reason of their suitability. Or else, under this heading, all the others are implicitly included.

Therein, clear comprehension of purposefulness is the discernment of a worthwhile purpose (in the action of looking ahead), without looking ahead at once following the impulse of the mind when the thought "I will look ahead" has arisen. This can be understood through the example of the venerable Nanda. For the Exalted One has said: "*Bhikkhus*, if Nanda thinks he should look to the east, he looks to the east after having attended to it fully with his mind, thus: 'When I look to the east, may no evil unwholesome states of mind such as covetousness and grief assail me.' Thus he is clearly comprehending in that action. If Nanda thinks he should look to the west … to the north … to the south … upwards … downwards … to an intermediate direction, he does so after having attended to it fully with his mind, thus: 'When I look to an intermediate direction, may no evil unwholesome states of mind such as covetousness and grief assail me.' Thus he is clearly comprehending in that action" (AN 8:9/AN IV 167).

SUB.CY. At the time of practicing insight meditation, the venerable Nanda thought to himself: "Because of not guarding the doors of the sense faculties, I fell into such a misfortune as discontent with the Buddha's dispensation, etc., I will control them thoroughly." Thus he became enthusiastic, acquired a strong sense of shame and moral dread, and as a consequence attained the highest perfection in the restraint of the senses. Thus the Teacher set him up as the chief disciple in that respect: "*Bhikkhus*, among all my disciples who are *bhikkhus*, the chief in guarding the doors of the sense faculties is Nanda" (A I 25).

CY. Further, clear comprehension of purposefulness and of suitability here should be understood by way of the previously mentioned examples of going to see a *cetiya*, etc. Clear comprehension of the resort is simply the non-relinquishing of the meditation subject. Therefore, those practicing here with the aggregates, elements, and sense bases as their meditation subjects should look ahead and look aside by way of their own meditation subject; those practicing such meditation subjects as the *kasiṇas* should look ahead and look aside keeping their meditation subject in mind.

SUB. CY. The purport is that no means other than the meditation subject such as the aggregates, etc., should be sought for.

CY. Clear comprehension of non-delusion here (in regard to looking ahead and looking aside) is understanding thus: "Internally there is no self which looks ahead and looks aside. When the thought 'Let me look ahead' arises, the mind-originated air element arises together with that thought, producing intimation. Thus, through the diffusion of the air element (resulting from) mental activity, the lower eyelid sinks down and the upper eyelid rises up; there is no one who, as it were, opens them up with a device. Then eye-consciousness arises accomplishing the task of seeing."

N. SUB. CY. The above passage is stated to show that since the one who looks ahead, etc., is a particular process of mere phenomena, clear comprehension of non-delusion is the understanding of that process in accordance with actuality.

"Through the diffusion of the air element (resulting from) mental activity": by way of bodily intimation, that is, the mode of motion pertaining to the air element originating from the mind, which consists of (mental) activity.

CY. Further, clear comprehension of non-delusion here should also be understood by way of the full understanding of the root (*mūlapariññā*), adventitiousness (*āgantukatā*), and temporariness (*tāvakālikabhāva*).

(1) *The full understanding of the root*

Life continuum and adverting,
Seeing and then receiving,
Investigating and determining
With impulsion in the seventh place.

Therein, the life continuum occurs accomplishing its task as the factor of rebirth-existence. When that breaks off, a functional mind element arises accomplishing the task of adverting; when that has ceased, an eye-consciousness arises accomplishing the task of seeing; when that has ceased, a resultant mind element arises accomplishing the task of receiving; when that has ceased a resultant mind-consciousness element arises accomplishing the task of investigating; when that has ceased, a functional mind-consciousness element arises accomplishing the task of determining; when that has ceased, impulsion impels seven times.[51] In this process, looking ahead and looking aside because of lust, hatred, and delusion governed by the thought "This is a woman, this is a man" do not occur in the first or second impulsion, or even in the seventh impulsion. But when these have broken up and fallen in sequence, below and above, like soldiers on a battlefield, it is then that looking ahead and looking aside occur because of lust, hatred, and delusion governed by the thought "This is a woman, this is a man." Thus clear comprehension of non-delusion should first be understood here by way of the full understanding of the root.

N. SUB. CY. The "full understanding of the root" is fully understanding the root-cause of mind-door impulsion. The

---

51. This passage gives a capsule statement of the cognitive series (*cittavīthi*) on an occasion of sense consciousness. The life continuum (*bhavaṅga*), the factor responsible for the coherence of personality, occurs for three moments before it breaks off and yields to the sense-door adverting consciousness, which begins the cognition of the outer sense object. The series reaches culmination in the seven occasions of impulsion (*javana*), which is followed by two occasions of registration consciousness (*tadārammaṇa*, not mentioned here) before giving way again to the life continuum.

life continuum occurs "accomplishing its task as the factor" because it is the principal factor (of existence) and it is the principal factor because of its similarity to the rebirth-linking consciousness. Or it occurs "accomplishing the task of the causal factor," because it is the cause for the uninterrupted occurrence (of the life process).

"In this process … even in the seventh impulsion": this is said because, in a cognitive process occurring through the five sense doors, there is no lust, hatred, and delusion governed by the thought "This is a woman, this is a man." For when the adverting and determining (states of consciousness) occur in an unwise mode because of unwise attention which occurred prior to adverting and determining, impulsion arises merely accompanied by greed in the case of a desirable object, such as the form of a woman, and merely accompanied by hate in the case of an undesirable object; but there is no extreme occurrence of lust and hatred, etc. It is only in the mind door that extreme lust and hatred, etc. occur. However, the impulsion (in the cognitive process occurring) through the five sense doors is the root of the lust and hatred occurring in the mind-door process; or else all the aforementioned states of consciousness, the life continuum, etc., (are the root). Thus the full understanding of the root is spoken of by way of the root-cause of mind-door impulsion, but adventitiousness and temporariness by way of the prior nonexistence and the evanescence, respectively, of the sense-door impulsions themselves.

"But when these have broken up and fallen in sequence, below and above": this means by way of the successive arisings of the life continuum. For the breaking up and falling of these (states of consciousness) occur by way of the arising of the life continuum. By this the commentator shows, by way of the successive arisings of the life continuum below (i.e. prior to the sense cognition) and above (i.e. subsequent to the sense cognition), the arising of the mind-door impulsion which is different from the sense-door impulsion. Because lust, etc., occur by way of that (mind-door impulsion), the commentator says: "It is then that looking ahead and looking aside occur because of lust, hatred, and delusion governed by the thought 'This is a woman, this is a man.'"[52]

(2) *Adventitiousness*

CY. When a form has come into the range of the eye door, after the vibrating of the life continuum, the adverting (and subsequent states of consciousness) arise and cease each accomplishing its own task; at the end, impulsion arises. That impulsion is like a visitor (*āgantukapuriso*) at the eye door, which is the house belonging to the previously arisen states of consciousness, such as adverting, etc. Just as it is not proper for a stranger who has entered the house of others in order to ask for something to issue commands when the owners of the house are sitting silently, so it is not proper for that impulsion to be lustful, hating, and deluded in the eye door—which is the house belonging to the states of consciousness such as adverting, etc.—when those states of consciousness themselves are without lust, hatred, and delusion. Thus clear comprehension of non-delusion should be understood by way of adventitiousness.[53]

N. SUB. CY. The eye door is called "the house belonging to the states of consciousness, such as adverting, etc." because it is the cause for their occurrence, since they occur when a form comes into the range of the eye door.

"Like a visitor": visitors are twofold—guests and chance arrivals. A guest is an acquaintance, a chance arrival is a stranger; the latter is intended by the analogy here.

52. The point of this long discussion is that because the greed and hate that arise in the sense-door cognitive processes lack the force that those same defilements acquire with their occurrence in mind-door cognitive processes, the application of clear comprehension to the sense experience can cut off the defilements and prevent them from gathering momentum in the mind-door process.

53. Since the defilements do not occur in the preliminary states of consciousness leading up to the *javana* stage, they are compared to unwelcome visitors who show up unexpectedly at the sense doors.

(3) *Temporariness*

CY. Those states of consciousness (beginning with adverting and) ending with determining which arise in the eye door, those break up together with their associated phenomena right on the spot (where they arose). They do not see one another. Thus they are evanescent and temporary. Therein, when all the people living in a single house have died, it is not proper for the sole survivor, being subject to die that very moment, to delight in singing and dancing; in the same way, when at a single sense door the states of consciousness such as adverting, etc., along with their associated phenomena have died right on the spot (where they arose), it is not proper for the survivor—that is, impulsion—being subject to die that very moment, to delight by way of lust, hatred, and delusion. Thus clear comprehension of non-delusion should be understood by way of temporariness.[54]

Further, this [clear comprehension of non-delusion] should be understood by way of reviewing the aggregates, sense bases, elements, and conditions. Herein, the eye and forms belong to the aggregate of materiality; seeing to the aggregate of consciousness; the associated feeling to the aggregate of feeling; perception to the aggregate of perception; contact, etc., to the aggregate of mental formations. Thus looking ahead and looking aside are discerned in the assemblage of these five aggregates. Therein, who is it that looks ahead? Who looks aside?

N. SUB. CY. Looking ahead and looking aside being discerned by way of the five aggregates, who is it, separate from those aggregates, that looks ahead? Who looks aside? The meaning is: there is no one who looks ahead, no one who looks aside.

CY. So, too, the eye is the eye base; form is the form base; seeing is the mind base; the associated phenomena such as

54. This method of clear comprehension involves reflecting that since all the occasions of consciousness leading up to the *javana* state have shown themselves to be impermanent, the mind in the *javana* stage should be cognizant of its own impermanence and should not allow itself to be governed by the defilements.

feeling, etc., are the mind-object base. Thus looking ahead and looking aside are discerned in the assemblage of these four sense bases. Therein, who is it that looks ahead? Who looks aside?

So, too, the eye is the eye element; form is the form element; seeing is the eye-consciousness element; the associated phenomena such as feeling, etc., are the mind-object element. Thus, looking ahead and looking aside are discerned in the assemblage of these four elements. Therein, who is it that looks ahead? Who looks aside?

So, too, the eye is a support condition [for seeing]; forms are an object condition; adverting is a proximity, contiguity, decisive support, absence, and disappearance condition; light is a decisive support condition; feeling, etc., are conascence conditions. Thus looking ahead and looking aside are discerned in the assemblage of these conditions. Therein, who is it that looks ahead? Who looks aside?[55]

Thus clear comprehension of non-delusion here should also be understood by way of reviewing the aggregates, sense bases, elements, and conditions.

3. On Bending and Stretching

ON BENDING AND STRETCHING THE LIMBS, HE ACTS WITH CLEAR COMPREHENSION

CY. This refers to the bending and stretching of the joints. Therein, clear comprehension of purposefulness is the discernment of a worthwhile purpose after examining to determine whether or not a worthwhile purpose can be achieved by means of bending and stretching the arms and legs; one does not bend and stretch the limbs following the impulse of the mind. Examining to determine whether or not a worthwhile purpose can be achieved should be understood as

55. For a concise but authoritative explanation of the different types of conditions admitted in the *Abhidhamma*, see Ledi Sayādaw, *The Buddhist Philosophy of Relations* (BPS Wheel No. 331/333).

follows. If one stands bending or stretching the arms and legs for too long a time, painful feelings arise moment by moment; the mind does not gain one-pointedness, one's meditation subject falls away, and one does not achieve distinction. But if one bends the limbs at the proper time and stretches them at the proper time, those painful feelings do not arise; the mind becomes one-pointed, one's meditation subject succeeds, and one achieves distinction.

Clear comprehension of suitability is the discernment of suitability, after examining to determine what is suitable and what is unsuitable even when there is a worthwhile purpose. Therein, this is the method of explanation:

On the terrace of the Great *Cetiya*, it is said, young *bhikkhus* were holding a recitation of the *Dhamma* while young *bhikkhunis* stood behind them listening. Then one young *bhikkhu*, stretching back his arm, came into bodily contact with one of the *bhikkhunis*, and by reason of that, he became a layman. Another *bhikkhu*, stretching out his leg, extended it into a fire, and his foot was burnt right down to the bone. Still another stretched his leg into an anthill, and he was bitten by a poisonous snake. Another stretched his hand out onto the pole of a tent, and a ribbon snake bit him. Therefore, one should not stretch out one's limbs when it is unsuitable, but should stretch them out only when it is suitable. This is clear comprehension of suitability.

Clear comprehension of the resort can be illustrated by the story of the Great Elder. The Great Elder, it is said, was sitting in his day-quarters talking with his pupils when he quickly bent in his arm; thereupon he returned his arm to its original position and again bent it in slowly. His pupils asked him, "Venerable sir, having bent in your arm quickly, why did you return it to its original position and again bend it slowly?" He replied, "Friends, from the time I started to attend to a meditation subject, never before have I abandoned my attention to it while bending in my arm. But now, while talking with you, I did so. Therefore I returned my arm to its original position and again bent it in." "Good, venerable sir, that is how a *bhikkhu* should be."

Thus here, too, clear comprehension of the resort should be understood simply as the non-relinquishing of the meditation subject.

Clear comprehension of non-delusion here (in regard to bending and stretching) should be understood as understanding thus: "Internally there is no self which bends and stretches. Bending and stretching occur, as aforesaid, through the diffusion of the air element (resulting from) mental activity, just as the arms and legs of a puppet move when their strings are pulled."

4. On Wearing Robes

ON WEARING HIS ROBES AND CLOAK AND USING HIS ALMSBOWL, HE ACTS WITH CLEAR COMPREHENSION

CY. Herein, "wearing his robes and cloak" means putting on his lower robe and upper robes, "using his almsbowl" means using the bowl to receive almsfood, etc. Therein, clear comprehension of purposefulness should be understood by way of the purpose in each case stated by the Exalted One: in wearing one's robes and cloak, when putting on the lower robe and upper robe and walking for alms (one reflects that) material gains are only "for protection from cold," etc.[56]

Clear comprehension of suitability should be understood as follows. A thin robe is suitable for one who is weak or whose body is naturally hot; a thick double-layered robe is suitable for one whose body is sensitive to cold. Their opposites are unsuitable. A worn-out robe is unsuitable for everyone, as it creates an impediment when it needs to be patched and sewn, etc. Robes of silk and fine cloth, etc., are also unsuitable since they stimulate greed. For one living alone in the forest, such robes may create an obstacle to his dwelling or to his life. But in the strict sense

56. Reflecting wisely, he uses the robe only for protection from cold, for protection from heat, for protection from contact with gadflies, flies, wind, burning and creeping things, and only for the purpose of concealing the private parts" (MN 2/M I 10). See Vism I. 86–88, pp. 31–32.

any robe that has been acquired by means of wrong livelihood, such as hinting, etc., and any robe that causes unwholesome states to increase and wholesome states to diminish when one uses it—that robe is unsuitable. The opposite of this is suitable.

Clear comprehension of the resort should be understood as the non-relinquishing of the meditation subject.

Clear comprehension of non-delusion here should be understood by way of the following line of reflection: "Internally there is no self which puts on the robes. The putting on of the robe occurs, as aforesaid, through the diffusion of the air element (resulting from) mental activity. Therein, the robe is insentient and the body is insentient. The robe does not know 'The body is covered by me,' and the body does not know 'I am covered by the robe.' Mere elements cover a collection of elements, like strips of cloth covering a mannequin. Therefore, if one gains a quality robe one should not become joyful, and if one gains a poor quality robe one should not become sad.

"Some people honor an anthill inhabited by a cobra, a tree shrine, etc., with garlands, perfume, incense, and cloths, etc.; others desecrate them with filth, urine, and mud and by striking them with rods and swords. Yet because of this, the anthill, the tree shrine, etc., do not become joyful or sad. In the same way if one gains a fine quality robe one should not become joyful, and if one gains a poor quality robe one should not become sad."

SUB. CY. By the phrase "the body is insentient" the commentator demonstrates that the body, like the robe, is empty of self. Explaining thus, he shows the reason for being content with whatever one gets.

CY. In using the almsbowl, clear comprehension of purposefulness should be understood by way of the purpose in what is to be obtained by taking the bowl. One does not grab the almsbowl suddenly, but reflects: "Having taken this, walking on almsround, I will gain almsfood."

Clear comprehension of suitability should be understood as follows. For one whose body is thin and weak, a heavy bowl is unsuitable; a bowl that has been cracked and repaired in four or five places and is difficult to wash is unsuitable for everyone. A bowl difficult to wash is not proper, and is an impediment for the one who washes it. A jewel-colored bowl stimulates greed and is thus unsuitable through the method stated in the case of robes. A bowl gained by (means of wrong livelihood such as) hinting, etc., and whatever bowl causes unwholesome states to increase and wholesome states to diminish when one uses it—this is extremely unsuitable. The opposite of this is suitable.

Clear comprehension of the resort should be understood as the non-relinquishing of the meditation subject.

Clear comprehension of non-delusion here should be understood by way of the following line of reflection: "Internally there is no self which takes the almsbowl. The taking of the almsbowl occurs, as aforesaid, through the diffusion of the air element (resulting from) mental activity. Therein, the bowl is insentient and the hand is insentient. The bowl does not know 'I have been taken by the hands,' and the hands do not know 'The bowl has been taken by us.' Mere elements take a collection of elements, like tongs taking a red-hot bowl."

Further, when kindhearted persons see other people lying abandoned in a home for the destitute—their arms and legs cut off, pus, blood, and maggots oozing from their open wounds, their bodies covered by bluebottle flies—they bring them bandages and medicines in bottles, etc. Some of the patients get soft bandages, others get coarse bandages; some get well-shaped medicine bottles, others get badly shaped medicine bottles. However, the patients do not become joyful or sad because of that, for they need bandages simply to cover their wounds and bottles simply to hold their medicine. Analogously, the *bhikkhu* who regards his robe as a bandage, his almsbowl as a medicine bottle, and the almsfood placed in the bowl as medicine in the bottle should be understood as the supreme practitioner of clear comprehension through clear comprehension of non-delusion in wearing the robes and using the almsbowl.

5. On Eating and Drinking

ON EATING, DRINKING, CHEWING AND TASTING, HE ACTS WITH CLEAR COMPREHENSION

CY. Here "eating" applies to soft foods, "drinking" to drinks such as congee, etc., "chewing" to hard foods such as pastries, and "tasting" to things which are tasted such as honey, molasses, etc.

In each case the purpose is eightfold, stated by way of the standard formula for reflecting on the use of almsfood.[57] Clear comprehension of purposefulness should be understood by way of that.

Clear comprehension of suitability should be understood as follows. Any kind of food which causes one discomfort, whether it be coarse or delicious, bitter or sweet, etc., is unsuitable. Any food which has been obtained by way of hinting, etc., and any food which causes unwholesome states to increase and wholesome states to diminish when one eats it—that is extremely unsuitable. The opposite of this is suitable.

Clear comprehension of the resort should be understood as the non-relinquishing of the meditation subject.

Clear comprehension of non-delusion should be understood by way of the following line of reflection: "Internally there is no self which eats. The receiving of the almsbowl occurs, as aforesaid, through the diffusion of the air element (resulting from) mental activity. Through the diffusion of that same air element (resulting from) mental activity, the hand is placed in the bowl, the food is formed into a lump, the lump is lifted to the mouth, and the mouth is opened. There is no one who opens the jaws with grease or a device. It is again through the diffusion of the air element (resulting from) mental activity that the lump is

---

57. "Reflecting wisely, he uses almsfood neither for amusement nor for intoxication nor for smartening nor for embellishment, but only for the endurance and continuance of this body, for the ending of discomfort, and for assisting the life of purity" (MN 2/M I 10). See Vism I. 89–92, pp. 32–33.

placed in the mouth, the upper teeth perform the work of a pestle, the lower teeth the work of a mortar, and the tongue the work of a hand. Thus the food is smeared with the thin spittle at the tip of the tongue and the thick spittle at the root of the tongue. When it has been stirred around by the tongue's hand in the mortar of the lower teeth, moistened by spittle, and pulverized by the pestle of the upper teeth, there is no one who makes it enter within with a spoon or ladle; it enters due to the air element itself. As each piece enters, there is no one who supports it on a straw mat; it remains there due to the air element. While it remains there, there is no one who builds an oven, lights a fire, and cooks each piece of food; the food is digested due to the heat element itself. And when it is digested, there is no one who expels each piece of waste with a stick or pole; it is expelled due to the air element itself.

"Thus the air element takes the food up [to the mouth], takes it down [to the stomach], supports it, rotates it, pulverizes it, dehydrates it, and expels it. The earth element supports it, rotates it, pulverizes it, and dehydrates it. The water element moistens it and maintains its wetness. The heat element digests it when it has entered within. The space element provides the passage ways [through which the food enters, rotates, and gets expelled]. The consciousness element, in accordance with the appropriate effort, attends to one thing or another."

N. SUB. CY. "The consciousness element" is mind-consciousness element, since the cognizing of the search for food, the eating of it, etc., is intended. "To one thing or another": to the tasks of searching for food, eating it, etc. "In accordance with the appropriate effort": the effort to accomplish each of those tasks, which becomes the condition for the cognizing of them. For the effort with which one accomplishes the search for food, etc., also accomplishes the cognizing which has that (action) as its objective domain, since the effort is indispensable to the cognizing.

"Attends": It adverts to and cognizes the searching for food, the eating of it, the digested or undigested state, etc., by way of experiencing the search, the eating, and the digested or undigested state, etc. Or else "the appropriate effort" means right practice, and "attends" means one reflects: "Internally there is no self which eats," etc.

CY. Further, clear comprehension of non-delusion here should be understood by way of reviewing the ten aspects of repulsiveness in food, thus: in terms of going, searching, eating, secretion, the receptacle, the undigested state, the digested state, fruit, outflow and smearing. The detailed explanation of this should be understood through the "Description of the Perception of Repulsiveness in Nutriment" in the *Visuddhimagga* (XI, 1-26, pp. 372–80).

N. SUB. CY. "Going": going towards the village which is one's alms resort in order to walk on almsround; returning, since it pertains to going, is also included in this. "Searching": wandering for alms in the village; this includes turning back and entering the alms-hall, etc., since these also pertain to searching. "Eating": when one is eating food which has been pulverized by the pestle of the teeth, at the time it is being stirred around by the tongue it has become extremely disgusting like dog's vomit in a dog's tray, a peculiar compound devoid of its (original) color and smell.

"Secretion": the four secretions—bile, phlegm, pus and blood—located above the stomach; when the food that has been eaten approaches these secretions, they cause it to become extremely disgusting.

"The receptacle": the stomach, so called because as the food is eaten, it accumulates and remains here. "The undigested state": the state of not being fully digested by the *kamma*-born heat responsible for digesting the food that has been eaten. "The digested state": the state of being fully digested by the aforesaid *kamma*-born heat.

"Fruit": its outcome, that is, its purpose. For when the food that has been eaten is properly digested, it produces the repulsive parts of the body such as head hairs, etc.; when it is not properly digested, it produces such illnesses as skin eruptions etc.

"Outflow": the discharge of waste through the numerous doors such as the eyes, ears, etc. For it is said:

"The food and drink so highly relished,
The hard that's chewed, the soft that's swallowed,
All enter through a single door
But through nine doors come flowing out."

"Smearing": at the time of eating, the hands, lips and other parts of the body get completely smeared with food; after eating, the nine doors get smeared.

In all these ways one should review the repulsiveness in food.

6. On Defecating and Urinating

On defecating and urinating, he acts with clear comprehension

CY. Therein, if one does not defecate and urinate when the time comes, sweat breaks out from one's entire body, one's eyes reel, the mind does not become one-pointed, and various kinds of illness arise. But if one does so, none of this happens. That is the purpose here, and clear comprehension of purposefulness should be understood by way of that.

If one defecates or urinates in an improper place, one falls into a disciplinary offence, acquires a bad reputation, and may meet an obstacle to life. But if one defecates and urinates in a proper place, none of this happens. That is what is suitable here, and clear comprehension of suitability should be understood by way of that.

Clear comprehension of the resort should be understood as the non-relinquishing of the meditation subject.

Clear comprehension of non-delusion should be understood by way of the following line of reflection: "Internally there is no self which defecates and urinates. Defecation and urination occur through the diffusion of the air element (resulting from) mental activity. Just as, when a boil comes to a head, it bursts open and pus and blood come out without any will; and just as, when a water vessel is excessively full, water comes out without any will—in the same way, when excrement and urine have accumulated in the bowels and the bladder, they are pressed out by the force of the air element and come out without any will. The excrement and urine which have thus come out do not belong to the *bhikkhu* himself or to anyone else; they are merely bodily excretions. How is that? It is the same as when dirty water is thrown out from a waterpot: it does not belong to the one who throws it out himself or to others, but is merely old washing water.

N. SUB. CY. "They come out without any will" (*akāmatāya*). This is said to reject the foolish conceptions that there is a self which makes them come out, and that they come out through the will of that self. What is meant is that they come out solely through the diffusion of the air element, without any desire or effort of a self.

7. On the Minor Postures

ON GOING, STANDING, SITTING, LYING DOWN, WAKING UP, SPEAKING, AND REMAINING SILENT, HE ACTS WITH CLEAR COMPREHENSION

CY. The postures of long duration are explained in the following *sutta*: "When going, a *bhikkhu* understands 'I am going'; when standing, he understands 'I am standing'; when sitting, he understands 'I am sitting'; when lying down, he understands 'I am lying down'" (MN 10/I 56–57).

Those of middling duration were explained above with the words: "In going forward and returning, in looking ahead and looking aside, in bending and stretching the limbs, he acts with clear comprehension." But here, with the words, "in going, standing, sitting, lying down, and waking up," the minor casual postures are explained. Therefore, in these cases too, activity with clear comprehension should be understood in the way stated.

However, the Elder Tipiṭaka Mahāsiva explains as follows. One who, having gone a long way or walked back and forth (in meditation) for a long time, afterwards stands and reflects thus: "The material and mental phenomena which occurred at the time of walking back and forth have ceased here"—he is called one who acts with clear comprehension in going.

One who, having stood for a long time while making a recitation, answering a question, or attending to a meditation subject, afterwards sits and reflects thus: "The material and mental phenomena which occurred at the time of standing have ceased here"—he is called one who acts with clear comprehension in standing.

One who, having sat for a long time while making a recitation, etc. afterwards rises and reflects thus: "The material and mental phenomena which occurred at the time of sitting have ceased here"—he is called one who acts with clear comprehension in sitting.

One who, while lying down making a recitation or attending to a meditation subject, falls asleep and afterwards rises and reflects thus: "The material and mental phenomena which occurred at the time of sleeping have ceased here"—he is called one who acts with clear comprehension in lying down and waking up. For sleep is the non-occurrence of active states of consciousness; wakefulness is their occurrence.

One who, while speaking, speaks mindfully and clearly comprehends, "This sound is produced in dependence on the lips, teeth, tongue, palate, and the appropriate effort of the mind"—he is called one who acts with clear comprehension in speaking. Or one who, having made a recitation, explained the *Dhamma*, expounded a meditation subject, or answered a question over a long time, afterwards becomes silent and reflects thus: "The material and mental phenomena arisen at the time of speaking have ceased here"—he too is called one who acts with clear comprehension in speaking.

One who, having silently attended to the *Dhamma* or to a meditation subject for a long time, afterwards reflects thus: "The material and mental phenomena which occurred at the time of being silent have ceased here; one speaks when there is a process of derivative materiality [i.e. the sound base] and is silent when there is no such process"—he is called one who acts with clear comprehension in remaining silent.

This explanation by the Elder Mahāsiva, with its emphasis on non-delusion, is intended in the Great Discourse on the Foundations of Mindfulness (*Mahāsatipaṭṭhāna Sutta*). But in this Discourse on the Fruits of Recluseship all four kinds of clear comprehension obtain. Therefore, acting with clear comprehension should be understood here by way of the four kinds of clear comprehension, in the way explained above.

N. SUB. CY. In the Elder Mahāsiva's explanation, acting with clear comprehension is understood by way of seeing the cessation, right on the spot, of the material and mental phenomena which occurred in each immediately preceding posture; therefore (his explanation of acting with clear comprehension) should be understood by way of the practice of insight, the clear comprehension of non-delusion that has come down in the Great Discourse on the Foundations of Mindfulness, not by way of the fourfold analysis of clear comprehension. Hence that explanation is the one intended there (in the Great Discourse on the Foundations of Mindfulness), not here (in the Discourse on the Fruits of Recluseship). Because the chief purpose of this teaching is to show the distinctive fruits of recluseship, here all four kinds of clear comprehension obtain. Therefore that is the meaning here (in the Discourse on the Fruits of Recluseship).

CY. When it is said (in the *sutta*) "he acts with clear comprehension," in all phrases the meaning should be understood by way of clear comprehension *associated with mindfulness.* For this passage (of the *sutta*) is a detailed explanation of the phrase "he is endowed with mindfulness and clear comprehension." Further, in the *Vibhaṅga* these phrases are analyzed thus: "Mindful and clearly comprehending he goes forward; mindful and clearly comprehending he returns," etc. (Vibh § 525/250–51).

N. SUB. CY. "Clear comprehension associated with mindfulness": by this the commentator shows that just as the importance of clear comprehension is understood through its function, so too in the case of mindfulness. But this does not show the mere presence of mindfulness along with clear comprehension, for knowledge never occurs devoid of mindfulness.

To explain why the meaning should be understood by way of clear comprehension associated with mindfulness, the commentator says: "For this passage (of the *sutta*) is a detailed explanation of the phrase 'he is endowed with mindfulness and clear comprehension.'" Thus, because the passage elaborates upon the meaning of a phrase which mentions both together, it can be accepted that, as in the synopsis, so in the exposition both mindfulness and clear comprehension are present with equal importance.[58]

To establish that point by the method of the *Vibhaṅga* as well, the commentator says: "Further, in the *Vibhaṅga*," etc. By this he demonstrates the importance here of mindfulness, just like that of clear comprehension. In the *Vibhaṅga* "these phrases"—the phrases of the exposition such as "in going forward and returning he acts with clear comprehension," etc.—"are analyzed," that is, they are analyzed separately in all cases, without subsuming mindfulness under clear comprehension.

The *Majjhima* reciters, however, and the *Ābhidhammikas* say thus: One *bhikkhu* while going, goes reflecting on one thing, thinking of another; another *bhikkhu* goes without relinquishing his meditation subject. Similarly while standing, sitting, and lying down, one lies down reflecting on one thing, thinking of another, another lies down without relinquishing his meditation subject. But to this extent, (they say), clear comprehension of the resort is not evident, illustrating their point by the example of the walkway (for practicing walking meditation).

For a *bhikkhu*, having entered the walkway, stands at the end of the walkway and discerns: "The material and mental phenomena which occurred at the eastern end of the walkway ceased right there, without reaching the western end of the walkway; those which occurred at the western end of the walkway ceased there, without reaching the eastern end of the walkway; those which occurred in the middle of the walkway ceased there, without reaching either end. The material and mental phenomena which occurred while walking back and forth ceased there, without reaching the standing posture; those which occurred while standing ceased there, without reaching the sitting posture; those which occurred while sitting ceased

58. The synopsis (*uddesa*) is the phrase "the bhikkhu (is) endowed with mindfulness and clear comprehension"; the exposition (*niddesa*) is the rest of the passage which details the way he acts with clear comprehension.

there, without reaching the lying posture." Discerning thus again and again, he falls asleep; when he rises, he rises taking up his meditation subject. This *bhikkhu* is called one who acts with clear comprehension in going, etc.

When one is asleep, the meditation subject becomes indistinct; but the meditation subject should not be made indistinct. Therefore, having walked back and forth, stood, and sat (in meditation), when lying down, in so far as he is able the *bhikkhu* lies down discerning thus: "The body is insentient; the bed is insentient. The body does not know 'I am lying on a bed'; the bed does not know 'A body is lying on me.' 'An insentient body is lying on an insentient bed.' Discerning thus again and again, his mind falls asleep; when he awakens, he awakens taking up his meditation subject. He is called one who acts with clear comprehension in going to sleep.

A *bhikkhu* who discerns thus: "Impulsion, or everything which occurs through the six doors, is a process consisting in activity, because it consists in that bodily activity, etc., by which it is produced, and because it is originated by the activity of adverting; when that exists, waking up occurs"—he is called one who acts with clear comprehension in waking up. Further, one who divides the day and night into six portions and remains awake during five portions is also called one who acts with clear comprehension in waking up.

One who teaches the *Dhamma* because it is a basis for liberation, and one who abandons the thirty-six kinds of frivolous chatter and speaks suitable talk based on the ten subjects of talk—he is called one who acts with clear comprehension in speaking.[59]

One directing attention to whichever among the thirty-eight objects of meditation is congenial to himself, and one who has attained the second *Jhāna*—he is called one who acts with

59. For the thirty-six kinds of frivolous chatter (*tiracchāna-kathā*), see §52 of the sutta above. The ten (suitable) subjects of talk are: wanting little, contentment, seclusion, aloofness from contact, arousing energy, moral discipline, concentration, wisdom, liberation, knowledge and vision of liberation (MN I 145/M III 113).

clear comprehension in remaining silent. For the second *Jhāna*, because it is devoid of verbal formations, is especially called silence.

IN THIS WAY, GREAT KING

CY. The meaning is: "In this way, undertaking (such actions as) going forward, etc., by way of clear comprehension associated with mindfulness, he is endowed with mindfulness and clear comprehension."

Contentment (*Santosa*)

66. HEREIN, GREAT KING, A *BHIKKHU* IS CONTENT WITH ROBES TO PROTECT HIS BODY AND ALMSFOOD TO SUSTAIN HIS BELLY

CY. He is endowed with contentment with requisites of any kind. This contentment is twelvefold. In regard to the robe there are three types of contentment: contentment which accords with one's gains, contentment which accords with one's strength, and contentment which accords with what is proper.[60] The same three types apply to almsfood and the other requisites (dwelling and medicine). Now follows the analytical explanation.

(1) *Robe*. Herein, a *bhikkhu* gains a robe, which may be of a fine quality or a poor quality. He maintains himself with that robe and does not wish for another one. This is his contentment with a robe which accords with his gains.

Another *bhikkhu* is physically weak, or he is afflicted with illness or old age, so that he feels tired when he wears a heavy robe. Thus he exchanges robes with a congenial *bhikkhu*, and is content maintaining himself with a light robe. This is his contentment with a robe which accords with his strength.

Another *bhikkhu* gains requisites of excellent quality. Having gained a valuable bowl or robe, or having gained many bowls and robes, he gives them away, thinking: "This is fitting

60. *Yathālābhasantosa, yathābalasantosa, yathāsāruppasantosa.*

for elders long gone forth; this is fitting for those who are highly learned; let this be given to sick *bhikkhus*, this to those who gain little." He himself takes their old robe, or he collects patches of cloth from a refuse heap and makes a robe, and is content wearing it. This is his contentment with a robe which accords with what is proper.

(2) *Almsfood.* Herein, a *bhikkhu* gains almsfood, which may be coarse or excellent. He maintains himself with that food and does not wish for any other kind; even if he gains something else he does not accept it. This is his contentment with almsfood which accords with his gains.

Another *bhikkhu* gains almsfood which does not agree with his physical constitution or with his health, so that if he were to eat it he would become ill. Thus he gives that food to a congenial *bhikkhu* and, having eaten suitable food received from the latter, he is content doing the work of a recluse. This is his contentment with almsfood which accords with his strength.

Another *bhikkhu* gains much excellent almsfood. As in the case of the robe, he gives it to elders long gone forth, to the highly learned, to those who gain little, and to the sick, and is content eating their leftovers; or having walked for alms, he is content eating various types of food mixed together (in his bowl). This is his contentment with almsfood which accords with what is proper.

(3) *Dwelling.* Herein, a *bhikkhu* gains a dwelling, which may be pleasant or unpleasant. He does not give rise to joy or sadness on that account, but is satisfied with whatever he gains, even with a straw mat. This is contentment with a dwelling which accords with his gains.

Another *bhikkhu* gains a dwelling which does not agree with his physical constitution or with his health, so that if he were to live there he would become ill. Thus he gives it to a congenial *bhikkhu* and is content living in a suitable dwelling belonging to the latter. This is his contentment with a dwelling which accords with his strength.

Another *bhikkhu*, one of great merit, gains many excellent dwelling places—caves, pavilions, gabled houses, etc. As in the case of the robe, he gives them away to elders long gone forth, to the highly learned, to those who gain little, and to the sick, and is content living anywhere. This is his contentment with a dwelling which accords with what is proper.

Again, a *bhikkhu* may reflect: "An excellent dwelling is a basis for heedlessness. While sitting there, one falls into dullness and drowsiness. One dozes off and when one awakens sensual thoughts arise." Having reflected thus, he does not accept any such dwelling, not even one which may fall to him. He refuses it and is content living in the open air or at the foot of a tree, etc. This, too, is his contentment with a dwelling which accords with what is proper.

Medicine.[61] Herein, a *bhikkhu* gains medicine, which may be coarse or excellent. He is satisfied with what he gains and does not wish for any other kind; even if he gains something else he does not accept it. This is his contentment with medicine which accords with his gains.

Another who needs oil gains molasses. He gives it to a congenial *bhikkhu* and, having gained oil from him or having sought for it elsewhere, he is content using it as medicine. This is his contentment with medicine which accords with his strength.

Another *bhikkhu*, one of great merit, gains much excellent medicine—oil, honey, molasses, etc. As in the case of the robe, he gives it away to elders long gone forth, to the highly learned, to those who gain little, and to the sick, and is content maintaining himself with whatever they bring him. If they were to put gall nuts and cow's urine in one vessel and a blend of the four sweets in another vessel, and say to him, "Venerable sir, take whatever you want"—supposing both were capable of curing his illness—he would think: "Medicine of gall nuts and cow's urine is praised by the Buddhas." Thus he would refuse the four sweets and be supremely content using gall nuts and cow's urine as medicine. This is his contentment with medicine which accords with what is proper.

---

61. The word *gilānapaccaya* includes, besides medicine proper, refreshments allowable for bhikkhus after midday, such as sugar, honey, and oil.

A *bhikkhu* endowed with this twelvefold "contentment with requisites of any kind" may make use of eight requisites: three robes, and almsbowl, a knife for cutting toothwood, a needle, a waistband, and a water-strainer.

All these have the purpose of "protecting one's body" and "sustaining one's belly." How? If, when one travels about, one wears the three robes, one sustains and protects the body; thus these are for protecting the body. If, when drinking, one first strains the water with a corner of a robe, or uses a robe to accept fruits to be eaten, one sustains and protects the belly; thus these are for sustaining the belly.

The almsbowl is for protecting the body if one uses it to draw water when bathing or making plaster for one's hut; it is for sustaining the belly when one uses it to receive food at meal time.

The knife is for protecting the body if one uses it to cut toothwood or to smoothen the legs and surface of one's bed and chair or the poles of a tent; it is for sustaining the belly if one uses it to cut sugarcane or to open a coconut, etc.

The needle is for protecting the body when one uses it to sew robes; it is for sustaining the belly if, at the time of eating, one uses it to pick up a piece of fruit or cake.

The waistband is for protecting the body when one puts it on before travelling about; it is for sustaining the belly if one uses it to bind and gather sugarcane, etc.

The water-strainer is for protecting the body when one strains water with it at the time of bathing or making plaster for one's dwelling; it is for sustaining the belly when one uses it to strain drinking water or to accept sesame seeds, rice grains, or honey-tree fruits while eating.

This is the limit of requisites for one using eight requisites. But for one using nine requisites, when he stays in a bedroom, a bedspread situated there or a key is allowed. For one using ten requisites, a sitting couch or a piece of leather is allowed. For one using eleven requisites, a walking stick or an oil tube is allowed. For one using twelve requisites, an umbrella or a pair of sandals is allowed.

It should not be said that, of these *bhikkhus*, only the one who uses eight requisites is content, and that the others are not content, have many desires, and are difficult to support. For they, too, are content, have few desires, are easy to support, and light in their mode of living. However, the Exalted One did not explain this discourse by way of those *bhikkhus*; he explained it by way of the one who uses eight requisites. For this one wraps up his small knife and needle in his water strainer, puts the strainer inside his almsbowl, hangs the bowl over his shoulder, clothes himself in his three robes and waistband, and sets out happily wherever he wishes. There is nothing at all he has to turn back for and take. Thus, showing such a *bhikkhu's* light mode of living, the Exalted One says: "A *bhikkhu* is content with robes to protect his body and almsfood to sustain his belly," etc.

HE SETS OUT TAKING ONLY (HIS REQUISITES) ALONG WITH HIM

CY. He goes taking all his minimal eight requisites, carrying them on his body. He has no attachment or bondage to "my monastery, my cell, my attendant." He is like an arrow released from the bow or like an elephant in rut which has left the herd. Using whatever dwelling he likes—a jungle thicket, the foot of a tree, a wooded slope—he stands alone and sits alone; in all postures, he is alone, without a companion. Thus he conducts himself in a manner similar to that of the rhinoceros, as explained (in the Rhinoceros Sutta):

At home in the four quarters of the world,
harboring no aversion in one's heart,
content with anything one gets,
bearing all hardships undismayed—
one should walk alone like the rhinoceros. (Sn 42)

JUST AS A BIRD, WHEREVER IT GOES, FLIES WITH ITS WINGS AS ITS ONLY BURDEN.

CY. The Buddha next demonstrates this point with the simile of the bird. This, in brief, is the meaning: Having learned that in such and such a region there is a tree with ripened fruits, birds come from various directions and eat those fruits, picking and tearing at them with their claws, wings, and beaks. It never occurs to them, "This is for today's meal, that is for tomorrow's meal." When the fruits are finished they do not set up a guard around that tree, nor do they set up a feather, claw mark, or beak mark there; rather, they lose their concern for that tree, and each bird goes in whatever direction it wishes, flying off with its wings as its only burden. In the same way, the *bhikkhu* sets out wherever he wishes, without attachment and without concern. Hence it is said: "He sets out taking only (his requisites) along with him."

Abandoning Hindrances (*Nīvaraṇappahāna*)

(67) ENDOWED WITH THIS NOBLE AGGREGATE OF MORAL DISCIPLINE ... HE RESORTS TO A SECLUDED DWELLING

CY. What does the Buddha show by this? He shows the achievement of the requisites for living in the forest. For one who lacks these four requisites[62] does not succeed in his forest life. He would fall under the same category as animals or forest wanderers. The deities residing in the forest would think, "What is the use of living in the forest for such an evil *bhikkhu*?" They would make frightful sounds, strike him on the head with their hands, and make him flee. A bad reputation would also spread about concerning him: "Such and such a *bhikkhu*, having entered the forest, did this and that evil deed."

But one who has achieved these four requisites succeeds in his forest life. Reviewing his own moral discipline, he does not see any stain or blemish, and he arouses rapture. Exploring that rapture by way of its destruction and falling away, he enters upon the plane of the noble ones. The deities residing in the forest are satisfied and speak praise of him. His fame spreads widely, like a drop of oil put onto water.

---

62. Moral discipline, restraint over the sense faculties, mindfulness and clear comprehension, and contentment.

Therein, "secluded" means empty, that is, quiet and noiseless. It is referring to this that it is said in the *Vibhaṅga*: "Secluded": even if a dwelling is nearby, if it is not crowded with householders and monks, then it is secluded" (Vibh § 526/251). A dwelling (*senāsana*, lit. "bed and seat") is a place where one lies down and sits; it is a designation for bed and chair. Thus it is said: "'Dwelling': a bed is a dwelling, a chair is a dwelling, a cushion, a pillow, a dwelling place, a building with a sloping roof, a rectangular building with a gabled roof, a flat-roofed building, a natural cave, a multi-storeyed mansion, a circular house, a rock cave, a bamboo thicket, the foot of a tree, a pavilion—these are also dwellings.[63] Or any place to which *bhikkhus* return, all this is a dwelling" (Vibh § 527/251).

Moreover, dwellings become fourfold as follows: A dwelling place, a building with a sloping roof, a rectangular building with a gabled roof, a flat-roofed building, a natural cave—these are called dwelling-place dwellings. A bed, a chair, a cushion, a pillow—these are called bed-and-chair dwellings. A rug, a piece of leather, a straw mat, a mat of leaves—these are called spread dwellings. "Or any place to which *bhikkhus* return"—this is called a living space dwelling. All these are included under the term "dwelling."

Here, however, the Buddha is showing the dwelling appropriate for a *bhikkhu* who is similar to a bird, at home in all four quarters of the world; then he says "he resorts to a secluded dwelling." Therein, "a forest": in the case of *bhikkhu*nis, a forest is explained as everything beyond the pillar marking the boundary of a village, but for the *bhikkhu* described here, it is fitting for his forest dwelling to be at least five hundred bow-lengths from the village. Its characteristics are explained in the *Visuddhimagga*, in the "Description of the Ascetic Practices" (II. 47–55, pp. 72–74).

"The foot of a tree" is the foot of any secluded tree having cool shade. "A mountain" is a rock mountain. For when one has

63. The translation of several one-word terms used in the Cy. incorporate the explanations provided by the Sub. Cy.

bathed and drunk in a rock tank and sits down in the cool shade of a tree, fanned by a cool breeze, the various quarters all visible, the mind becomes one-pointed.

"A glen" is a mountainous region divided by water; some say it is a place where rivers rush and roar. For there the sand is like silver foil; the jungle thicket overhead is like a jewel-studded canopy, and the water flows like a mass of jewels. Having entered such a glen, drunk and cooled one's limbs, heaped up sand and prepared a seat from rag-robes, when one sits down and does the work of a recluse, the mind becomes one-pointed.

"A hillside cave" is a large fissure between two mountains or in a single mountain similar to a tunnel. The characteristics of a cremation ground are explained in the *Visuddhimagga* (II.64-68, pp. 76-78). "A jungle grove" is a place beyond the outskirts of a village, a place not frequented by men, where they do not sow and plough. Thence it is said: "'A jungle grove': this is a designation for remote dwellings." "The open air": an uncovered place. One wishing to may make a tent and live here. "A heap of straw": a pile of straw. For having collected straw from a large heap of straw, they build an abode similar to a hillside cave. They also throw straw over bushes and brush, etc., sit beneath it, and do the work of a recluse.

HE SITS DOWN, CROSSES HIS LEGS, HOLDS HIS BODY ERECT, AND SETS UP MINDFULNESS BEFORE HIM

CY. "(He) crosses his legs": he binds them with the thighs completely locked. "(He) holds his body erect": he sets the upper part of his body erect, aligning the eighteen vertebrae end to end. For when one sits in such a way, the skin, flesh, and sinews do not bend forward, and the painful feelings which might arise moment after moment because of their being bent forward do not arise. As those feelings do not arise, the mind becomes one-pointed and the meditation subject does not fall away, but arrives at growth, success, and maturity.

"(He) sets up mindfulness before him": he applies mindfulness towards his meditation subject; or he sets it up in the region of the mouth. Thus it is said in the *Vibhaṅga*: "This mindfulness is set up, set up well, at the tip of the nose or at the sign of the mouth" (Vibh § 537/252).

N. SUB. CY. The "sign of the mouth" (*mukhanimitta*) is the middle region of the upper lip, against which the air strikes when it comes out of the nose.

68. HAVING ABANDONED COVETOUSNESS FOR THE WORLD

CY. Here the five aggregates of clinging are the world (*loka*), in the sense of decaying (*lujjana*) and disintegrating (*palujjana*). Therefore the meaning here is: having abandoned lust for the five aggregates of clinging, having suppressed sensual desire.

"He dwells with a mind free from covetousness": with a mind free from covetousness through its being abandoned by way of suppression, not like eye-consciousness [which is naturally devoid of covetousness].

"He purifies his mind from covetousness": he releases his mind from covetousness; he acts in such a way that he lets go of covetousness and does not grasp it again.

N. SUB. CY. Purification (of the mind) means acting in such a way that it is presently released and in the future is not taken up again. Just as his mind becomes free from covetousness through its being purified by the preliminary meditative development, so in the same way it becomes free from ill will, dullness and drowsiness, restlessness, and doubt.

CY. "Ill will": the mind is made ill by this, and abandons its original nature, like spoiled gruel. "Hatred": one is defiled by undergoing deformation (because of this), or one defiles and destroys others. Both these words ("ill will" and "hatred") are designations for anger. "Dullness" is sickness of the mind, "drowsiness" is sickness of mental factors; together they are called "dullness and drowsiness." "Perceiving light": he is endowed with a purified perception free from the hindrances, capable of perceiving, whether by day or by night, a light previously seen. "Mindful and clearly comprehending": he is endowed with mindfulness and knowledge; these two are mentioned because they are both helpful to the perception of light. He has "passed beyond doubt" in that he lives having crossed over and transcended doubt. He is "unperplexed about wholesome states" because, in regard to blameless states, he does not doubt: "Are these wholesome? How is it that these are wholesome?" This is a brief explanation. Whatever has to be said concerning these five hindrances—the analysis of their word derivations, characteristics, etc.—all has been said in the *Visuddhimagga*.

> 74. WHEN A *BHIKKHU* SEES THAT THESE FIVE HINDRANCES ARE UNABANDONED WITHIN HIMSELF, HE REGARDS THAT AS A DEBT, AS A SICKNESS, AS CONFINEMENT IN PRISON, AS SLAVERY, AS A DESERT ROAD

CY. Here the Exalted One shows the unabandoned hindrance of sensual desire as similar to a debt, and the remaining hindrances as similar to sickness, etc. The similarity is as follows.

One who has taken a loan from others and squandered it cannot defend himself when they tell him to pay back his debt, speak to him harshly, bind him and beat him; he must endure this all, and his debt is the reason he must endure it. Similarly, if someone becomes excited by sensual desire towards someone else and takes [that person] as an object of a mind associated with craving, then he must endure it all when that person [the object of his sensual desire] speaks to him harshly, binds him and beats him; his sensual desire is the reason he must endure it. An example is the case of women being beaten by the house-owners [their parents-in-law, their sensual desire being the reason they must endure it]. Thus sensual desire should be regarded as a debt.

One who is afflicted with a bile disease, if he is given such things as honey and sugar, will not enjoy their taste because of his bile disease. He will spit them out thinking they are bitter. Similarly, if one with a mind of ill will is exhorted even slightly by his benevolent preceptor or teacher, he will not accept the exhortation. He will reject it, saying "You oppress me too much!" and depart [either to wander about here and there or to return to lay life]. Just as the man afflicted with a bile disease cannot enjoy the taste of honey and sugar, so one afflicted with anger cannot enjoy the flavor of the Buddha's dispensation, that is, the happiness of *Jhāna*, etc. Thus ill will should be regarded as a sickness.

On a festival day a man bound in prison cannot see either the beginning, middle, or end of the festival. If he is released the next day, and he hears, "Oh, there was a delightful festival yesterday! Oh, such dances and songs!" he cannot give a reply. For what reason? Because he did not enjoy the festival himself. Similarly, if a *bhikkhu* is overcome by dullness and drowsiness when a preaching of the *Dhamma* through variegated methods is taking place, he cannot understand its beginning, middle, or end. When the preaching is over he hears others speaking praise of it, "Oh, what a preaching of the *Dhamma*! Such arguments and similes!" but he cannot give a reply. For what reason? Because he was overcome by dullness and drowsiness and did not enjoy the *Dhamma* talk. Thus dullness and drowsiness should be regarded as confinement in prison.

A slave, even when playing at a festival, may be told: "There is some urgent task for you to do. Go there quickly! If you don't go, I'll cut off your hands and feet, your ears or your nose!" Thus he goes quickly and does not get to enjoy the beginning, middle, or end of the festival. For what reason? Because he is subservient to others. Similarly, when one who is unskilled in the *Vinaya* has entered the forest for seclusion, he may incur some minor disciplinary offence, even perceiving unallowable meat as allowable. Then he has to abandon his seclusion and approach a master of the *Vinaya* to purify his moral discipline. Thus he does not get to enjoy the happiness of seclusion. Why? Because he has been overcome by restlessness and worry. Thus restlessness and worry should be regarded as slavery.

A man travelling along a desert road, having seen the opportunity for thieves to plunder and kill people, becomes anxious and frightened even by the sound of a twig or a bird, thinking "Thieves have come." He goes forward [a little], stops [because of his anxiety and fear], and turns back [thinking,

"Who knows what will happen if one travels in such a desert?"]. The places in which he stops are more numerous than those in which he walks. He reaches a place of safety with trouble and difficulty, or he may not reach it at all. Similarly, if doubt about the eight cases has arisen in someone, he will go on doubting "Is the Teacher an Enlightened One or not?" and will not be able to resolve (his doubts) and accept it in faith. Not being able to do so, he does not reach the path or fruit. Thus, just as the traveller on the desert road, by doubting whether or not there are thieves, repeatedly arouses wavering and vacillation, lack of conviction and consternation, and creates an obstacle to his reaching a place of safety, so by doubting whether or not the Teacher is an Enlightened One, one repeatedly arouses wavering and vacillation, lack of conviction and consternation, and creates an obstacle to one's reaching the plane of the noble ones. Thus doubt should be regarded as a desert road.

N. SUB. CY. The eight cases are stated in the *Vibhaṅga*, thus: "Therein, what is doubt? One doubts and distrusts the Teacher, the *Dhamma*, the *Saṅgha*, the training, the past, the future, the past and future together, and specifically conditioned, dependently arisen phenomena" (Vibh §915/365).

75. BUT WHEN HE SEES THAT THESE FIVE HINDRANCES HAVE BEEN ABANDONED WITHIN HIMSELF, HE REGARDS THAT AS FREEDOM FROM DEBT, AS GOOD HEALTH, AS RELEASE FROM PRISON, AS FREEDOM FROM SLAVERY, AS A PLACE OF SAFETY

CY. Here the Exalted One shows the abandoning of the hindrance of sensual desire as similar to freedom from debt, and the abandoning of the remaining hindrances as similar to good health, etc. The similarity is as follows.

A man, having taken a loan, applies it to his business and achieves success. He thinks, "This debt is a root impediment," so he pays back the loan together with the interest and has the promissory note torn up. From then on no one sends him a messenger or a letter (reminding him of his debt). When he sees his creditors he may rise up from his seat or remain seated, as he wishes. Why? Because he is no more bound to them, no more dependent on them. Similarly, a *bhikkhu* thinks, "Sensual desire is a root impediment," so he develops six things and abandons the hindrance of sensual desire. When he has thus abandoned sensual desire, then just as a man free from debt experiences no fear or consternation when he sees his creditor, so the *bhikkhu* experiences no attachment or bondage towards any external object. Even if he sees divine forms no defilement assails him. Therefore the Exalted One says that the abandonment of sensual desire is like freedom from debt.

N. SUB. CY. The six things to be developed (for abandoning sensual desire) are: learning the sign of the unattractive (that is, the repulsive nature of the body), application to meditation on the unattractive, guarding the doors of the sense faculties, moderation in eating, noble friendship, and suitable talk.[64]

CY. A man afflicted with a bile disease suppresses that disease with a preparation of medicines. From then on he enjoys the taste of such things as honey and sugar. Similarly, a *bhikkhu* thinks, "Ill will is a major cause of harm," so he develops six things and abandons the hindrance of ill will. When he has thus abandoned ill will, then just as the man who has recovered from the bile disease eats such things as honey and sugar and relishes their taste, so the *bhikkhu*, having respectfully received the training rules such as the promulgations concerning conduct, etc., trains himself in them and relishes them. Therefore the Exalted One says that the abandonment of ill will is like good health.

N. SUB. CY. The six things to be developed (for abandoning ill will) are: learning the sign of loving kindness, application to meditation on loving kindness, reflection on the ownership of action, abundance of wise reflection, noble friendship, and suitable talk.

CY. A man is placed in prison on a festival day. On a later festival day he thinks, "Previously, due to my own heedlessness,

64. For a fuller discussion of the six things conducive to the abandoning of each hindrance, see *The Way of Mindfulness*, pp. 119–129.

I was bound in prison, and thence I did not enjoy the festival. Now I will be heedful." Thus he becomes heedful, so that his foes do not get the chance (to have him imprisoned). Having enjoyed the festival, he utters the joyful exclamation, "Oh, what a festival! Oh what a festival!" Similarly, a *bhikkhu* thinks, "Dullness and drowsiness are a major cause of harm," so he develops six things and abandons the hindrance of dullness and drowsiness. When he has thus abandoned dullness and drowsiness, then just as the man freed from imprisonment enjoys the beginning, middle, and end of the festival even for a week, so the *bhikkhu* enjoys the beginning, middle, and end of the festival of *Dhamma*, and attains *arahatship* together with the analytical knowledges (*paṭisambhidā*). Therefore the Exalted One says that the abandonment of dullness and drowsiness is like release from prison.

N. SUB. CY. The six things to be developed (for abandoning dullness and drowsiness) are: recognizing that overeating is the basis (for dullness and drowsiness), changing the postures, attention to the perception of light, living in the open air, noble friendship, and suitable talk.

CY. A slave, with the help of a friend, gives money to his master and frees himself from slavery. From then on he can do whatever he wishes to. Similarly, a *bhikkhu* thinks, "Restlessness and worry are a major cause of harm." so he develops six things and abandons the hindrance of restlessness and worry. When he has thus abandoned restlessness and worry, then just as a free man can do whatever he wishes to and no one can forcibly prevent him from doing so, so the *bhikkhu* happily practices the way of renunciation, and restlessness and worry cannot forcibly prevent him from doing so. Therefore the Exalted One says that the abandonment of restlessness and worry is like freedom from slavery.

N. SUB. CY. The six things are: much learning, interrogation, skill in the *Vinaya*, associating with senior monks, noble friendship, and suitable talk.

CY. A strong man, having taken his valuables in hand, might travel through a desert fully armed, accompanied by his retinue.

Thieves, having seen him even from afar, would flee. Having safely crossed the desert and arrived at a place of safety, he would become joyful and exuberant. Similarly, a *bhikkhu* thinks, "Doubt is a major cause of harm," so he develops six things and abandons the hindrance of doubt. When he has thus abandoned doubt, then just as the strong man fully armed, accompanied by his retinue, is fearless, and taking no more account of thieves than of grass, safely leaves the desert and arrives at a place of safety, so the *bhikkhu* crosses the desert of misconduct and arrives at the supreme place of safety—the deathless, the great *Nibbāna*. Therefore the Exalted One says that the abandonment of doubt is like a place of safety.

N. SUB. CY. The six things are: much learning, interrogation, skill in the *Vinaya*, resolution, noble friendship, and suitable talk.

76. When he sees that these five hindrances have been abandoned within himself, gladness arises

CY. "Gladness arises": the quality of joy (*tuṭṭhākāra*) arises. "When he is gladdened, rapture arises": for one who is joyous, rapture arises, shaking his entire body.

"When his mind is filled with rapture, his body becomes tranquil": for a person whose mind is associated with rapture, his mental body becomes tranquil; it becomes free from disturbance. "He experiences happiness": he experiences bodily and mental happiness. "His mind becomes concentrated": for one who enjoys this happiness of renunciation, the mind becomes concentrated by way of access and by way of absorption.

N. SUB. CY. "The quality of joy": by this the commentator shows tender rapture. For, due to its tenderness, that (rapture) at the stage of joy is simply the quality of joy.

"For one who is joyous": the subcommentary says, "for one who is joyous by way of rapture that has reached the showering state." In such a case, the term "gladness" may be understood to mean "showering rapture" (*okkantikā pīti*). "Rapture arises, shaking his entire body": the subcommentary explains, as the meaning of this, that rapture characterized by pervasion arises, shaking the entire body by its own pervasiveness and by producing excellent material phenomena originated by itself. In such a case, the term "rapture" may be understood to mean "pervading rapture" (*pharaṇā pīti*). The shaking of the body here is the production of a current of rapture, a pervasion of rapture throughout the entire body.

"Mental body" (*nāmakāya*): here the entire cluster of immaterial phenomena is intended, not the three mental aggregates (exclusive of consciousness)—feeling, perception, and mental formations—as is intended by the phrase "agility of body" (*kāyalahutā*), etc., nor the material body, as is intended by the phrase "the body (as) a sense base" (*kāyāyatana*), etc. The tranquillizing is intended by way of the two kinds of tranquillity (of consciousness and of the other three mental aggregates). "Free from disturbance": free from disturbance by the defilements; this means that disturbance by such defilements as restlessness, etc., has been abandoned.

"He experiences bodily and mental happiness": by means of the aforementioned preliminary meditative development he experiences mental happiness, and because his body has been suffused by the excellent material phenomena originated by that (mental happiness), he also experiences bodily happiness.

"This happiness of renunciation" (*nekkhammasukha*): the happiness of access concentration is called renunciation because it has departed from the faction of defilements and hindrances, and the happiness of absorption is called renunciation because it pertains to the first *Jhāna*. As concentration takes place here in both ways, it is said "by way of access and by way of absorption."

Herein, this is the purport. The phase from the abandonment of sensual desire up to the experiencing of happiness by one tranquil in body, as previously too, is said to be the preliminary meditative development, not absorption. But in the case when the mind of one who is happy becomes concentrated, both preliminary concentration and absorption concentration are intended, for happiness is the cause for absorption just as it is for the development of access, and because the absorption to be described in the formula for the first *Jhāna* is achieved by means of the cause-and-effect relationship. Or else, like the preliminary happiness, the happiness of absorption is also a cause for absorption concentration; thus the Teacher Dhammapāla accepts the happiness of absorption as a cause for absorption concentration.

The *Jhānas*

77. Quite secluded from sense pleasures ... He enters and Dwells in the first *Jhāna*

CY. This is said in order to show the higher distinctions when the mind is concentrated by access concentration, and to show the divisions of concentration when the mind is concentrated by absorption concentration.

N. SUB. CY. In the last section of the *sutta* it was said: "Happy, his mind becomes concentrated." This states the concentrating of the mind by way of both access concentration and absorption concentration. In such a case the question may be raised: "What is the purpose of the teaching that begins 'Quite secluded from sense pleasures,' etc.?" The commentator gives the above statement as the answer.

"In order to show the higher distinctions": that is, in order to show the distinctions to be attained: the first *Jhāna*, etc., which are higher than access concentration, and the second *Jhāna*, etc., which are higher than the first *Jhāna*. For such distinctions as the first *Jhāna*, etc., can be achieved only through the achievement of access concentration, not without it, and the sequence of causes such as gladness, etc., is recognized as necessary for the achievement of the second *Jhāna* too.

"To show the divisions of concentration": with regard to that concentration characterized as absorption, and spoken of in general terms thus, "happy, his mind becomes concentrated"—to show the analysis of that into the second *Jhāna*, etc., and into the first direct knowledge, etc.

He drenches, steeps, saturates, and suffuses his body with this rapture and happiness born of seclusion

CY. "He drenches": he moistens; he extends rapture and

happiness everywhere. "Steeps": he applies all around. "Saturates": he fills as if filling a bellows with air. "Suffuses": he pervades all around. "His body": the material body composed of the four elements.

"There is no part of his entire body": in this *bhikkhu's* body, with all its parts, in the place where the kammically acquired material continuity occurs there is not even the slightest place consisting of skin, flesh and blood which is not suffused by the happiness of the first *Jhāna*.

In the simile for the second *Jhāna*, the material body is like the lake and the happiness of the second *Jhāna* is like the water.

SUB. CY. In the simile for the third *Jhāna*, the material body is like the lotuses and the happiness of the third *Jhāna* is like the water.

CY. In the simile for the fourth *Jhāna*, the white cloth is mentioned for the purpose of showing suffusion by heat. For there is no suffusion by heat with a soiled cloth; with a clean cloth that has just been washed the suffusion by heat is strong. For in this simile the material body is like the cloth and the happiness of the fourth *Jhāna* is like the suffusion by heat. Therefore, just as when a man has bathed well and is sitting covered from the head down by a clean cloth, the heat from his body suffuses the entire cloth so that there is no part of the cloth not suffused by heat, similarly, there is no part of the *bhikkhu's* material body that is not suffused by the happiness of the fourth *Jhāna*. It is in this way that the meaning should be seen here.

N. SUB. CY. *Query*: Isn't it true that by the statement "there would be no part of his entire body not suffused by the white cloth," the text speaks of the suffusion of the body by the white cloth, but not of the suffusion of the cloth by heat? Then why (in the commentary) is the suffusion by heat spoken of here?

Reply: Anticipating this inquiry, the commentator says, "For in this simile," etc. What is meant is that the meaning should be understood in the way explained (by the commentator) because the material body is like the cloth and the happiness of the fourth *Jhāna* is like the suffusion by heat. By this he shows that by mentioning the body the cloth which rests upon it should be understood, and by mentioning the cloth the suffusion by heat which occurs by reason of the cloth is intended; (for otherwise) the simile could not connect with the object of comparison and it is impossible for the entire body to be suffused by a white cloth.

This simile has been stated with a meaning that requires interpretation (*neyyatthato*), for the Exalted Buddha's teachings are variegated. The meditator's material body should be regarded as similar to the cloth because it is to be suffused by the happiness of the fourth *Jhāna*, which is similar to the suffusion by heat. The happiness of the fourth *Jhāna* is like the suffusion by heat because it is to suffuse the meditator's material body, which is like the cloth. The man's body (in the simile) is like the fourth *Jhāna* itself because the *Jhāna* is the basis for the happiness just as (the man's body is the basis) for the suffusion by heat. Thus the commentary says "Therefore," etc., for this demonstrates the correctness of the previous statement. And here, when it is said in the text, "with a pure bright mind," by mentioning mind the Exalted One refers to the happiness of the fourth *Jhāna*. To indicate this the commentary mentions the happiness of the fourth *Jhāna* twice.

Query: But isn't it true that in the fourth *Jhāna* there is no happiness having the characteristic of comfort (*sātalakkhaṇa*)? [65]

Reply: That is true. But here equanimity itself, because of its peacefulness, is intended by the word "happiness." Hence it is said in the *Sammohavinodanī* (the commentary to the *Vibhaṅga*): "Because of its peacefulness, equanimity is spoken of as happiness" (Vibh-a 171).

CY. A step-by-step explanation of the four *Jhānas*, and of the method of developing them, is given in the *Visuddhimagga*. Thus they are not explained in detail here.

It should not be thought that at this point only the one who gains the material-form *Jhānas* has been shown, but not the one who gains the immaterial *Jhānas*. For there can be no

65. This question is raised because in the fourth jhāna happiness, as pleasant feeling, is absent, having been replaced by equanimous feeling which is neither painful nor pleasant.

achievement of the higher direct knowledges without achieving mastery in fourteen ways over the eight meditative attainments. In the text only the material-form *Jhānas* have come down, but the immaterial *Jhānas* should be brought in and explained.

N. SUB. CY. This is said because the eight meditative attainments are indispensable to the achievement of the direct knowledges.[66] The 'fourteen ways' are: (i) in the forward order of the *kasiṇas*, (ii) in the reverse order of the *kasiṇas*, (iii) in the forward and reverse order of the *kasiṇas*, (iv) in the forward order of the *Jhānas*, (v) in the reverse order of the *Jhānas*, (vi) in the forward and reverse order of the *Jhānas*, (vii) skipping *Jhānas*, (viii) skipping *kasiṇas*, (ix) skipping *Jhānas* and *kasiṇas*, (x) transposition of factors, (xi) transposition of object, (xii) transposition of factors and object, (xiii) definition of factors, and (xiv) definition of object. These have been explained in the *Visuddhimagga* (XII, 3–7, pp. 410–11).

Even though the *Jhānas* have been mastered in the five ways—in adverting, etc. (see Vism, IV. 131, p. 160)—the fourteen kinds of mastery are recognized as essential for producing direct knowledge. The attainment (of direct knowledge) does not succeed by mastery over the material-form attainments alone, without mastery over the immaterial attainments. Thus the immaterial attainments are indispensable for achieving direct knowledge.

Query: If the immaterial *Jhānas* are to be included in the text, then why did the Exalted One give an elliptical account without mentioning them?

Reply: Because the fourth *Jhāna* of the material-form sphere is the special basis for all the direct knowledges. For even though (the immaterial *Jhānas*) are indispensable for the direct knowledges, the latter take the fourth *Jhāna* of the material-form sphere as their special basis. Therefore, in order to show that the fourth *Jhāna* is their basis, the teaching is presented stopping

66. That is, the five mundane kinds of direct knowledge shown in the sutta §89–98. Such mastery is not needed for the sixth, supramundane direct knowledge.

there (at the fourth *Jhāna*). But this does not mean that the immaterial *Jhānas* are unnecessary. Thus the commentator says: "The immaterial *Jhānas* should be brought in and explained."

Insight Knowledge (*Vipassanā-ñāṇa*)

85. WHEN HIS MIND IS THUS CONCENTRATED ... AND ATTAINED TO IMPERTURBABILITY

CY. He shows that the *bhikkhu* has achieved mastery over the eight meditative attainments in fourteen ways. The rest should be understood by the method explained in the *Visuddhimagga* (XII. 13-19, pp. 412–14).

HE DIRECTS AND INCLINES IT TO KNOWLEDGE AND VISION

CY. Here, "knowledge and vision" (*ñāṇadassana*) can mean path knowledge, fruition knowledge, the knowledge of omniscience, reviewing knowledge, or insight knowledge. In the passage, "What, friend, is the holy life lived under the Exalted One for the sake of purification of knowledge and vision?" (MN 24/M I 147), path knowledge is called "knowledge and vision." In the passage, "This is another superhuman state, a distinction in knowledge and vision worthy of the noble ones, a comfortable dwelling that has been achieved" (MN 31/M I 208), knowledge and vision is fruition knowledge. In the passage, "Then the knowledge and vision arose in the Exalted One that Āḷāra Kālāma had died seven days ago" (MN 26/M I 170), it is the knowledge of omniscience. In the passage, "And the knowledge and vision arose in me, 'Unshakable is my liberation, this is my last birth'" (MN 26/M I 167), it is reviewing knowledge. But here, when it is said, "He directs and inclines (his mind) to knowledge and vision," it is insight knowledge that is called "knowledge and vision."

"He directs and inclines it": he makes his mind slant, slide, and slope in order to produce insight knowledge.

"This is my body ... impermanent, subject to rubbing and pressing, to dissolution and dispersion"

CY. It is "impermanent" in the sense of not being after having been. It is "subject to rubbing" because it is anointed [with perfume, etc.] in order to remove its bad smell. It is "subject to pressing" because it is massaged to dispel ailments of the limbs; also, when children have limbs that have been misshapen during their stay in the womb, during infancy they are made to lie between the thighs and are pulled and pushed in order that their limbs may acquire the proper shape. It is "subject to dissolution and dispersion" because, though maintained in such ways, it is its very nature to break up and be scattered. Therein, six terms signify origination, the last two terms together with impermanence signify passing away.

N. SUB. CY. These nine terms (in the *sutta*) show the contemplation of the body as subject to origination and falling away. The six terms which signify origination are: having material form, composed of the four primary elements, originating from father and mother, built up out of rice and gruel, subject to rubbing, and subject to pressing.

Query: Admittedly, it is correct to say that the middle three terms signify origination, since they convey that meaning. But how can it be correct to say that the terms "having material form" and "subject to rubbing and pressing" signify origination when they do not convey that meaning?

Reply: It is correct, for they do convey that meaning. The term "having material form" conveys the meaning of "possessing material form," because material form includes temperature and nutriment, which serve as its own conditions.[67] The two terms, "subject to rubbing" and "subject to pressing," convey the meaning of acquiring the proper shape by producing the appropriate material form.

67. The reference is to the *Abhidhamma* teaching that temperature and nutriment, which are included in material form, are at the same time two of the four causes for the origination of material form, the other two being *kamma* and consciousness.

AND THIS IS MY CONSCIOUSNESS, SUPPORTED BY IT AND BOUND UP WITH IT

CY. Consciousness is supported by and bound up with the body composed of the four primary elements.

N. SUB. CY. This is said because the insight consciousness (*vipassanā-citta*) is supported by the heart basis included in the body. For it is only the insight consciousness then occurring that is known immediately by direct cognition thus, "This is my consciousness." It is "bound up" with the body because it does not occur without the body and because it takes as its object the material phenomena designated "the body."

86. CY. The application of the simile of the gem should be understood as follows. The gem is like the material body, and the thread running through it is like insight knowledge.[68] The man with keen sight is like the *bhikkhu* who gains insight. The time when the man takes the gem in his hand, reviews it, and clearly knows, "This is a gem"—this is like the time when the *bhikkhu* is sitting, having directed his mind to insight knowledge, and the body composed of the four primary elements becomes clear to him. The time when it becomes clear to the man, "This is a thread running through it"—this is like the time when the *bhikkhu* is sitting, having directed his mind to insight knowledge, and it becomes clear to him that the pentad inclusive of contact, or all states of consciousness and mental factors, or insight knowledge alone, take that as their object.[69]

N. SUB. CY. "Take that as their object" (*tadārammaṇānaṃ*): they take the material phenomena designated "the body" as their object. By mentioning the pentad inclusive of contact and all states of consciousness and mental factors, those phenomena comprised by the insight act of consciousness are included.

Query: Then why is the insight consciousness itself mentioned?

---

68. N. Sub. Cy. suggests the correct reading may be "insight consciousness" (*vipassanā-viññāṇa*).

69. The "pentad inclusive of contact" (*phassapañcamaka*): consciousness, feeling, perception, volition, and contact.

Reply: Because of the statement, "And this is my consciousness, supported by it and bound up with it," which may refer to that alone. For having seen with insight "This is my body," one attends to it as the support and objective domain (of insight consciousness) thus: "This very same consciousness associated with insight knowledge is supported by it and bound up with it." Therefore it is possible here to mention that alone and nothing else. Thus the commentator says "or insight consciousness alone."[70]

"The pentad inclusive of contact" is mentioned here because this is evident by the method taught in the *Dhamma*saṅgaṇī, etc.; "all states of consciousness and mental factors," in order to comprise everything relevant without omission; and "insight consciousness," because it is the principal factor in what is taught according to the letter.

CY. This insight knowledge immediately precedes the path, but even so it is shown here because there would be no intermediate place for it once the section on the direct knowledges has begun. It is also shown here in order to help one who has attained direct knowledge acquire the means for dispelling fear. For when one hears a fearful sound with the divine ear, or recollects fearful aggregates with the recollection of past lives, or sees a fearful form with the divine eye, fear and terror arise if one has not explored (formations) as impermanent, etc., but they do not arise if one has explored (formations) as impermanent, etc. Further, it is shown here at the beginning because the happiness of insight is a separate visible fruit of recluseship leading to the acquisition of the happiness of the paths and fruits.

N. SUB. CY. The criticism might be raised that, since insight knowledge immediately precedes the path, it should be mentioned after the mundane kinds of direct knowledge but before the sixth direct knowledge.[71] Then why is it mentioned prior to all the direct knowledges? The explanation that follows in the commentary is stated to remove that criticism.

---

70. So according to N. Sub. Cy., but Cy. itself reads "or insight knowledge alone."

71. The knowledge of the destruction of the cankers, which is supramundane.

"There would be no intermediate place for it": after the five mundane direct knowledges have been explained, the sixth direct knowledge must then be explained as is done in innumerable *sutta*s; for it has the characteristic of direct knowledge and is thus included in that category. But insight knowledge cannot be explained by inserting it in between the mundane kinds of direct knowledge and the sixth direct knowledge; for it lacks the characteristic of direct knowledge and is thus not included in that category. Thus there is no place for insight knowledge in between the direct knowledges. Because there is no opportunity for explaining it there, insight knowledge is explained here, immediately after the fourth *Jhāna* of the fine-material sphere.

"Sees a fearful form with the divine eye": here it can also be said, "When, with the physical eye, he sees a fearful form which he has created by the knowledge of supernormal power ...." For fear and terror arise in one who gains direct knowledge if he has not fully understood the basis,[72] as in the case of the Elder Mahānāga who resided at Uccavālika. The same can be said for one who, with the physical ear, hears a fearful sound which he has created by the knowledge of supernormal power, again as in the case of the Elder Mahānāga. For the Elder created (by supernormal power) an entirely white bull-elephant complete with trumpeting, and when he saw it and heard its sound, fear and terror arose in him.

Knowledge of the Mind-made Body
(*Manomay'iddhi-ñāṇa*)

87. HE CREATES ANOTHER BODY HAVING MATERIAL FORM, MIND-MADE, COMPLETE IN ALL ITS PARTS, NOT LACKING ANY FACULTIES

CY. "Mind-made" (*manomaya*): produced by mind. "Not lacking any faculties": not deprived of any faculties by way

72. That is, if he has not gained insight into formations as impermanent, suffering, and non-self.

of figure. For if the possessor of supernormal power is white, then the form he creates will also be white. If his earlobes are unpierced, the form will also have earlobes which are unpierced. Thus it is similar to him in all respects.

N. SUB. CY. "Not deprived of any faculties by way of figure" (*saṇṭhāna*): it is complete by way of the figures of the eyes, ears, etc. For the created form has no sensitivity (to sense objects). This statement shows that there is also no life faculty, etc., in the created form. "By way of figure": by way of the mere figure which (in the case of the eye) is similar to a lotus petal, not by way of the sense faculty which (in the case of the eye) is the sensitivity capable of receiving the impact of forms.

88. CY. The three similes are stated to show the similarity (of the mind-made body to its original). For the reed inside the sheath is similar to its sheath; the sword is similar to its scabbard, since they put a round sword into a round scabbard and a flat sword into a flat scabbard; the snake's slough is similar to the snake. Though in the text it is said, "Suppose a man were to pull a snake out from its slough," as if he were to pull it out with his hand, we should understand that he extracts it mentally. For no one can pull a snake out from its slough. A snake abandons its slough by itself alone, through four means: by abiding in the law of its species; by supporting itself against a log or a tree; by its strength, that is, the effort of dragging its body out from the skin; and by feeling disgust towards the old skin as if it were devouring its body. Thus the statement of the text should be understood to refer to the mental extraction of the snake.

The application of the similes here is as follows: the *bhikkhu's* body is similar to the sheath, etc., and the created form is similar to the reed, etc. But the method of creation here and the following five kinds of direct knowledge—the modes of supernormal power, etc.—have been explained in full detail in the *Visuddhimagga* (Chapters XII and XIII). Thus they should be understood by the method stated there; here only the similes are additional.

Knowledge of Modes of Supernormal Power
(*Iddhividha-ñāṇādi*)

90. CY. Therein, the skilled potter, etc., is like the *bhikkhu* who gains the knowledge of the modes of supernormal power, the well-prepared clay, etc., is like the knowledge of the modes of supernormal power, and the making of whatever kind of vessel, etc., he might desire is like the *bhikkhu's* transformations (by supernormal power).

92. CY. Since a desert road is fearful and dangerous, and one who becomes anxious and frightened there cannot distinguish the sounds of kettledrum and tambours, in the simile for the divine ear-element the Buddha does not mention a desert road, but with the word "highway" shows a safe road. For when one is travelling leisurely on a safe road free from dangers, having placed a cloth over one's head [to ward off wind and the heat of the sun], one can easily distinguish the aforesaid sounds. The time when the sounds being heard by the man become clear to him is like the time when the divine and human sounds, both distant and near, become clear to the meditator.

94. In the simile for the knowledge of encompassing the minds of others, just as the mark on a young man's face would become evident to him when he examines his facial reflection, so the sixteen states of mind of others become evident to the *bhikkhu* sitting with his mind directed to the knowledge of encompassing the minds of others.

96. In the simile for the knowledge of recollecting past lives, only the three villages gone to that same day are mentioned, for it is the actions done that day which are evident. Therein, the man who has gone to the three villages is like the one who gains the knowledge of recollecting past lives, the three villages like three existences. Just as the actions done that day in the three villages become clear to the man, so do the actions done in the three existences become evident to the *bhikkhu* sitting with his mind directed to the knowledge of recollecting past lives.

98. In the simile for the divine eye, the upper-terraced building in the central square is like the *bhikkhu's* material body, the man with

keen sight standing in the building like the *bhikkhu* who has attained the divine eye. Those entering a house are like those entering the mother's womb by way of relinking; those leaving the house are like those leaving the womb; those walking along the streets are like those beings who repeatedly wander [in *saṃsāra*]; those sitting in front, in the open air in the central square, are like the beings who have arisen here and there in the three realms of existence. The time when these people become clear to the man standing on the upper terrace of the building—this is like the time when the beings arisen in the three realms of existence become clear to the *bhikkhu* sitting with his mind directed to the knowledge of the divine eye. This statement is made for ease of teaching, but the immaterial realm does not come into the range of the divine eye.

SUB. CY. "For ease of teaching": only for ease of teaching, not because those beings who have arisen in the immaterial realm become clear to the divine eye. For if it were said "except for the immaterial realm of existence" or "in two realms of existence," the teaching would not be easy to understand.

Knowledge of Destruction of Cankers
(*Āsavakkhaya-ñāṇa*)

99. WHEN HIS MIND IS THUS CONCENTRATED ... HE DIRECTS AND INCLINES IT TO THE KNOWLEDGE OF THE DESTRUCTION OF THE CANKERS

CY. "When his mind is thus concentrated": here, the mind of the fourth *Jhāna* used as the basis for insight should be understood.

N. SUB. CY. Insight is threefold, according to the division of the individuals who develop insight: the insight of great *bodhisattas*, the insight of *paccekabodhisattas*, and the insight of disciples. For great *bodhisattas* and *paccekabodhisattas*, insight is a self-evolved knowledge developed from their knowledge born of reflection (*cintāmayañāṇa*). For disciples, insight originates from the instruction given by others and is developed from their knowledge born of learning (*sutamayañāṇa*). Explicated in the *Visuddhimagga* by diverse methods, the latter is manifold as shown in such passages as "he should emerge from any fine-material or immaterial *Jhāna*, except the base consisting of neither-perception-nor-non-perception" (XVIII.3, p. 679); again, it is manifold under the heading of the immaterial and under any heading among several headings for the discernment of the elements stated in the defining of the four elements (XI.27–117, pp. 380–406).

But the insight knowledge of great *bodhisattas* involves diverse methods which can be classified under twenty-four hundred thousand *koṭis* (*koṭi*=10,000,000) of headings. This knowledge, reaching full maturity, gives birth to the preliminary knowledge which serves as the foundation of the knowledge of the noble path, the latter being the support for (a Buddha's) omniscience. Spoken of in the commentaries as "the great diamond knowledge" (*mahāvajirañāṇa*), it is supremely deep, very fine and subtle, not shared in by others. The Teacher's twenty-four hundred thousand *koṭis* of daily habitual meditative attainments are spoken of as being entered upon as a basis for that insight knowledge, classified in twenty-four hundred thousand *koṭis* of ways through the analysis of its mode of occurrence. The movement of the Buddha's insight has been shown synoptically by the Teacher Dhammapāla in the *Paramatthamañjūsā*, his commentary on the *Visuddhimagga*. Those who are interested should consult that work. Here only the insight of disciples is intended.

CY. "He directs and inclines (his mind)": he makes the insight consciousness slant, slide, and slope in that direction.

"To the knowledge of the destruction of the cankers": for the purpose of producing the knowledge of the destruction of the cankers. And here the path, the fruit, *Nibbāna*, and dissolution are called the destruction of the cankers (*āsavakkhaya*). In the passage, "knowledge of destruction, knowledge of non-arising" (DN 33/D III 214), the path is called the destruction of the cankers. In the passage, "Through the destruction of the cankers one is a recluse" (MN 40/M I 284), it is the fruit. In the passage:

He who seeks another's faults,
Who is ever censorious—
His cankers grow. He is far
From the destruction of the cankers. (Dhp 253)

—it is *Nibbāna*. And in the passage, "The destruction of the cankers, their falling away, breakup, impermanence, and disappearance" (untraced), it is dissolution (*bhaṅga*). Here *Nibbāna* is intended; the path of *arahatship* is also appropriate.

HE UNDERSTANDS AS IT REALLY IS "THIS IS SUFFERING"

CY. He understands as it really is, by penetration of its specific essential characteristic, the entire truth of suffering thus, "There is this much suffering, and none beyond this." And he understands as it really is, by penetration of its specific essential characteristic, the craving which produces that suffering thus, "This is the origin of suffering"; and the state by the attainment of which both suffering and its origin cease, (namely) *Nibbāna*, their non-occurrence, thus, "This is the cessation of suffering"; and the noble path which brings about its attainment thus, "This is the way leading to the cessation of suffering."

N. SUB. CY. "By penetration of its specific essential characteristic" (*sarasalakkhaṇapaṭivedha*): the commentator shows that to understand "as it really is" means to understand by penetration of the specific essential characteristic. The essence (*rasa*) is the specific nature (*sabhāva*) which is to be "tasted" or known.[73] Something's own essence is its specific essence (*sarasa*), which is itself the characteristic. Thus (the above phrase) means: by the penetrating of that (characteristic) without delusion. And "penetrating of that (characteristic) without delusion" (in regard to the first noble truth) means the occurrence of knowledge in such a way that afterwards there is no delusion in delimiting the specific identity (*sarūpa*), etc., of the truth of suffering. Hence it is said: "he understands as it really is."

---

73. The word *rasa*, used in the commentaries to mean the essence, or often, the function of a thing, originally had the sense of taste, and is in fact so used in the suttas as the object of tongue-consciousness.

When it is said in the text, "This is suffering," in order to show that the noble truth of suffering has then been grasped by the *bhikkhu* through direct cognition after having been delimited and exhausted, the commentator says, "There is this much suffering, and none beyond it." By the first phrase he shows that it has been grasped after having been delimited, by the second that it has been grasped after having been exhausted. Hence he says "the entire truth of suffering." Craving is called "the origin of suffering" because suffering originates from it.

"The state by the attainment of which both suffering and its origin cease, (namely) *Nibbāna*": that is, (they cease) in dependence upon *Nibbāna*, which becomes a cause for the path in the sense of being its object condition. *Nibbāna* is called "their non-occurrence" either because it is the basis (*nimitta*) for their non-occurrence in the sense that because of it (*etena*) they no longer occur, or because it is the state (*ṭhāna*) of their non-occurrence in the sense that they do not occur there (*ettha*).

He understands as it really is: "These are the cankers"

CY. Having shown the truths in their specific identity, the Buddha speaks the following passage about the cankers to show them again figuratively by way of the defilements.[74]

SUB. CY. "By way of the defilements": that is, by way of the defilements consisting in the cankers. The word "figuratively" (*pariyāyato*) is used because the cankers are a figurative expression (*pariyāya*) for the truth of suffering, as they are included in it, and their origin, cessation, and way to their cessation are figurative expressions for the remaining truths, respectively. And the cankers alone are mentioned here [and not the other defilements] because the passage was undertaken in terms of the knowledge of the destruction of the cankers [not in terms the other defilements]. Thus, when it is said "his mind is

---

74. That is, the distinction is between the direct exposition of the Four Noble Truths in terms of suffering, and the indirect exposition in terms of the cankers.

liberated from the canker of sensual desire," etc., liberation from all the defilements is stated under the heading of liberation from the cankers.

KNOWING AND SEEING THUS ...

CY. The Buddha explains the path which has reached its peak, together with insight.

N. SUB. CY. As it was said, "He understands as it really is, 'This is suffering,'" etc., it is a mixed path that is explained here, since the supramundane path has been explained, mixed together with insight, which is mundane.[75]

HIS MIND IS LIBERATED ... FROM THE CANKER OF IGNORANCE. WHEN IT IS LIBERATED, THE KNOWLEDGE ARISES: "IT IS LIBERATED"

CY. By the phrase "his mind is liberated," the Buddha shows the moment of the path, by the phrase "when it is liberated" the moment of the fruit, and by the phrase "the knowledge arises: It is liberated" the moment of reviewing knowledge. By the passage "destroyed is birth," etc., he shows the plane of the reviewing knowledge; for when the one who has destroyed the cankers reviews (his achievement) with that knowledge, he understands, "Destroyed is birth," etc.

N. SUB. CY. By the phrase "knowing and seeing thus" three (of the four) breakthroughs were stated—those of full understanding, realization, and development. But the breakthrough of abandonment, which remains, is stated by the phrase "his mind is liberated." Thus the commentator says, "(by this) the Buddha shows the moment of the path." For the four tasks are accomplished by the understanding of the four truths.[76]

---

75. Insight (*vipassanā*) is called mundane (*lokiya*) because it is directed to understanding the truths of suffering and its origin, which are mundane. The path realizing Nibbāna is, like its object, supramundane (*lokuttara*).

76. The four "breakthroughs" (*abhisamaya*), which are the same as the four tasks (*kicca*), apply one each to each of the Four Noble Truths:

Another method of explanation, separate from that of the commentary, is this: "*Because* of knowing, *because* of seeing, his mind is liberated from the cankers." And here, though the acts of knowing and seeing are simultaneous with the event of being liberated, still (the distinction between) the condition and what is conditionally arisen obtains even for things that are simultaneous.

And here, when the canker of existence is mentioned, the view of existence is incorporated within it along with the lust for existence. Thus the canker of views should also be considered to be included.

He understands: "Destroyed is birth ... there is nothing further beyond this"

Cy. *Query*: What birth of his is destroyed? And how does he understand this? It is not a past birth that is destroyed, for that was already destroyed previously. It is not a future one, for there is no effort in regard to the future. And it is not the present one, because that presently exists.

Reply: It is the birth which would have arisen if the path had not been fully developed, consisting of one, four or five aggregates in one, four or five-constituent existence, respectively. By the fully developed state of the path, that birth is destroyed because it has become impossible for it to arise in the future. Having reviewed the defilements abandoned by the development of the path, he knows that in the absence of defilements, even though action occurs, it does not bring about relinking (by rebirth) in the future. Thus he understands, "Destroyed is birth."

N. SUB. CY. "It is not a past birth": the *bhikkhu's* past birth is not destroyed by the development of the path, for that was destroyed by way of ceasing prior to the development of the path. "It is not a future one": the inquirer says this for the purpose of demonstrating his criticism by a pretext, mentioning the future in general terms, not a particular future. What is meant is that

---

full understanding (*pariññā*) to the truth of suffering, abandonment (*pahāna*) to its origin, realization (*sacchikiriya*) to its cessation, and development (*bhāvanā*) to the path.

by the development of the path there can be no effort to destroy (what is) in the future, for effort occurs only in regard to what is presently existent, not in regard to what is presently nonexistent. But here (in the Buddha's statement) it is a particular future that is intended, and effort applies to the destruction of that. Thus the commentator says: "It is the birth which would have arisen,'" etc. By this, destruction is shown (to apply) in fact to a future birth, by means of the destruction of its cause—the defilements—through the development of the path.

CY. "The holy life has been lived": the holy life of the path has been fully lived. For the seven learners together with the good worldling are said to be *living* the holy life, the one with cankers destroyed *to have lived* the holy life. Therefore, reviewing his own living of the holy life, he understands: "The holy life has been lived."

"What had to be done has been done": the sixteen tasks have been completed by way of the full understanding, abandonment, realization and development of the Four Noble Truths by the four paths. The meaning is that the defilements to be abandoned by each path have been abandoned, and the root of suffering has been eradicated. For the good worldling, etc., are *doing* what has to be done; the one with cankers destroyed *has done* what had to be done. Therefore, reviewing what had to be done by himself, he understands: "What had to be done has been done."

"There is nothing further beyond this" (*nāparaṃ itthattāya*): he understands: "Now there is no task of developing the path to be done by me again *for this state*, that is, for the (completion of) the sixteen tasks or for the destruction of the defilements." Or else, "this" can be understood as (the ablative) "beyond this." Hence he understands: "*Beyond this* presently existing continuum of aggregates occurring in such a mode, there is for me no further continuum of aggregates. These five aggregates stand fully understood, cut off at the root like trees. With the cessation of the last state of consciousness, they will be extinguished like a fire without fuel and will go to the indescribable state."

N. SUB. CY. "For (completing) the sixteen tasks": the functions of the noble path—full understanding, etc.—are intended. For when one reviews the path, those appear evident through the spiritual power of the path, since the reviewing of those tasks is accomplished easily once the path has been reviewed. Having thus shown the sixteen tasks in general by way of the four tasks in each of the four paths, since abandonment is the primary task among them and the others have that as their purpose, to show it separately the commentator says "or for the destruction of the defilements."

In the second interpretation, "beyond this" has an ablative meaning. "Further" means "future." "These five aggregates" constituting the last individuality "stand fully understood," that is, they are known after having been delimited by the path. By this he shows that they are without a footing (*appatiṭṭhatā*). For those (aggregates) which are rooted in lack of full understanding have a footing. As it is said, "*Bhikkhus*, if there is lust for material food, delight in it and craving for it, consciousness gets a footing in it and sprouts" (SN 12:64/S II 101). To illustrate this with a simile he says "cut off at the root like trees." As trees which have been cut off at the root, because they lack a root, stand without a footing, without a hold, so too do these five aggregates the root of which has been fully understood.

"The indescribable state" (*apaṇṇattikabhāva*): a description is formed by ascription in diverse ways to presently existent aggregates. They "go to the indescribable state" (so called) because, when such (aggregates) are absent, there is no description applicable to it.

100. Great king, suppose in a mountain glen ...

CY. The time when the oyster-shells, etc., become clear to the man with keen sight standing on the bank seeing them—this is like the time when the Four Noble Truths become clear to the *bhikkhu* sitting having directed his mind to the knowledge of the destruction of the cankers.

At this point, ten kinds of knowledge have been expounded: insight knowledge, the knowledge of the mind-made body, the knowledge of the modes of supernormal power, the knowledge of the divine ear, the knowledge of encompassing the minds of others, the knowledge of recollecting past lives, the pair—the knowledge of the future and the knowledge of faring on in accordance with *kamma*—accomplished by means of the divine eye, the knowledge of the divine eye (itself), and the knowledge of the destruction of the cankers. The analysis of their objects should be known. Therein, insight knowledge has seven kinds of objects: limited and exalted, past, future and present, internal and external. The knowledge of the mind-made body takes as its object only the (mentally) created form base; thus its object is limited, present, and external. The knowledge of the destruction of the cankers has an object which is immeasurable, external, and not describable (by reference to time).[77] For the rest, the division of their objects has been explained in the *Visuddhimagga* (XIII. 102-29, pp. 471–78).

N. SUB. CY. Because the pair—the knowledge of the future and the knowledge of faring on in accordance with *kamma*—have not come down in the text, they are said to be "accomplished by means of the divine eye." What is meant is that, because they are accomplished by means of the divine eye, when the latter is mentioned these two knowledges are implicitly included. For these two knowledges are the auxiliaries of the divine eye. The knowledge of the divine eye is shown (in the text) under the name of the knowledge of passing away and reappearing.

AND, GREAT KING, THERE IS NO OTHER FRUIT OF RECLUSESHIP HIGHER OR MORE SUBLIME THAN THIS ONE

CY. The Exalted One concludes the teaching with its culmination in *arahatship* thus, "There is no fruit of recluseship better in any way than this one."

N. SUB. CY. He concludes the teaching on the fruits of recluseship, which is not shared in by others, which demonstrates the essencelessness of the opinions of the sectarian religious teachers, which dispels the diverse forms of wrong livelihood such as scheming

77. This object is Nibbāna, which is said to be "external" because it is not included among the personal five aggregates, not because it can be discovered with the physical senses.

and talking, etc., which is adorned with the three kinds of moral discipline, which explains the practice of the supreme effacement, which is ornamented with the superhuman states such as the *Jhānas* and direct knowledges, etc., and which is decorated with the fourteen great fruits of recluseship. Just as a house of gems culminates in the crest jewel, so he concludes the teaching with its culmination in *arahatship*, for the word "liberated" means that the fruit of *arahatship* has been taught.

Ajātasattu Declares Himself a Lay Follower

101. CY. Having listened carefully to the beginning, middle, and end of the discourse, applauding it here and there, the king thought: "For a long time I have asked the ordinary recluses and brahmins these questions, but as if threshing chaff, I did not gain anything essential. Oh, the Exalted One is endowed with such excellent qualities! He answers these questions of mine creating a great light, as if he were lighting a thousand lamps for me. For a long time I have been deceived, not knowing the spiritual power of the Buddha's excellent qualities!" As he thus recollected the excellent qualities of the Buddha, his body was suffused by the five kinds of rapture. Revealing his own confidence, he then declared himself a lay follower. To show this, the passage that begins "When the Exalted One had finished speaking" is undertaken.

EXCELLENT, VENERABLE SIR! EXCELLENT, VENERABLE SIR!

CY. The word "excellent" (*abhikkanta*) is used here as an expression of appreciation. An intelligent person repeats a phrase on occasions of fear, anger, praise, haste, excitement, astonishment, laughter, sorrow and confidence. Here, it should be understood, the repeated exclamation is stated by way of confidence and praise. Or else "excellent" means extremely lovely, extremely desirable, extremely pleasing, extremely good.

Here, by one exclamation of "excellent" the king extols the teaching, by the other his own confidence. This is the purport here: "Excellent, venerable sir, is the Exalted One's teaching of the *Dhamma*. Excellent is my confidence dependent on the Exalted One's teaching of the *Dhamma*."

Or else he extols the word of the Exalted One itself, referring in each case to a double meaning. Thus the statement may be interpreted as follows: "The word of the Exalted One is excellent because it destroys faults, excellent because it promotes the achievement of excellent qualities. Similarly, (it is doubly excellent) because it generates faith and generates wisdom, because it possesses meaning and is well phrased, because it is clear in terminology and deep in meaning, because it is pleasant to the ear and wins the heart, because it does not extol himself and does not disparage others, because it is cooled by compassion and cleansed by wisdom, because it is delightful to listen to and can withstand examination, because it is pleasant when heard and beneficial when investigated," and so on.

The king next extols the teaching with four similes. This is the interpretation of the purport: "Just as if one were to turn upright what had been turned upside down, so when I had turned away from the true *Dhamma* and had fallen into a false *Dhamma*, the Exalted One helped me to emerge from that false *Dhamma*. Just as if one were to reveal what was hidden, so the Exalted One has revealed the dispensation, which had been hidden by the jungle of wrong views from the time the dispensation of the Exalted Buddha Kassapa disappeared. Just as if one were to point out the right path to one who was lost, so when I was travelling along a false path, a wrong path, the Exalted One disclosed to me the path to heaven and to liberation. And just as if one were to bring a lamp into a dark place, so when I was submerged in the darkness of delusion and could not see the gem-like forms of the Buddha, the *Dhamma*, and the *Saṅgha*, the Exalted One brought me the lamp of the teaching, which dispels the darkness of delusion concealing those forms. Because the *Dhamma* has been revealed to me in these ways by the Exalted One, (I say:) 'the Exalted One has revealed the *Dhamma* in numerous ways.'"

I go for refuge to the Exalted One, to the *Dhamma*, and to the *Bhikkhu Saṇgha*

CY. Having thus extolled the teaching, expressing his confidence with a mind of confidence in the Triple Gem, he says: "I go for refuge to the Exalted One," etc. The meaning is: "The Exalted One is my refuge, my supreme resort, the destroyer of misery, the provider of welfare. With this intention I go to the Exalted One, I devote myself to him, I follow him, I attend upon him." Or else: "I know and understand (him to be) thus." This last explanation is given because (in the Pali language) verbal roots which have the meaning "going" (*gati*) also have the meaning "understanding" (*buddhi*). Therefore it is said that "I go" can also mean "I know, I understand."

The word "*Dhamma*" is derived from the verb "supports" (*dhāreti*), because it supports those who have achieved the path, who have realized cessation, who are practicing as instructed, preventing them from falling into the four planes of misery. In denotation, the *Dhamma* is the noble path and *Nibbāna*. For this has been said: "*Bhikkhus*, to whatever extent there are things (*dhammā*) which are conditioned, the Noble Eightfold Path is declared the best of them" (AN 4:34/A II 34).

The *Dhamma* is not only the noble path and *Nibbāna*, but also the scriptural *Dhamma* together with the noble fruits. For this is said in the "Story of the Heavenly Mansion of the Brahmin Youth Chatta":

> The fading of lust, the wishless and the sorrowless,
> The unconditioned state, attractive,
> Sweet, potent, well analyzed—
> This *Dhamma* I approach for refuge. (Vv 616)

Here, "the fading of lust" is the path; "the wishless and the sorrowless" is the fruit; "the unconditioned state" is *Nibbāna*; and the "attractive, sweet, potent, well analyzed" is the aggregates of *Dhamma* analyzed into the three Pitakas (*Vinaya*, Sutta, and *Abhidhamma*).

The *Saṅgha* consists of those who are united through unity of view and moral discipline. In denotation, it is the assembly of the eight noble individuals. For this is said in the "Story of Chatta":

> Those eight persons, seers of *Dhamma*,
> Those four purified pairs of men
> In whom gifts given bring great fruit—
> This *Saṅgha* I approach for refuge. (Vv 617)

The *Bhikkhu Saṅgha* is the *Saṅgha* of *bhikkhus*. To this extent the king has declared his threefold going for refuge.

SUB. CY. "United through unity of view and moral discipline" (*diṭṭhisīlasaṅghātena*): they are united in the view stated thus, "he dwells possessing in common (with his companions in the holy life) such a view as is noble and emancipating, as leads one who practices in accordance with it to the complete destruction of suffering" (MN 48/I 322); and in the moral discipline stated thus, "he dwells possessing in common (with his companions in the holy life) such moral discipline as is unbroken, untorn, unblotched, unmottled, freeing, praised by the wise, unclung to, conducing to concentration" (MN 48/I 322). Thus the meaning is: they possess view and moral discipline in common. For wherever noble individuals live, even at a distance, they are unified through the common harmony of their excellent qualities.

Going for Refuge (*Saraṇa-gamana*)

In order to gain proficiency with regard to (the subject of) going for refuge, the following method of exposition should be understood: (1) the (meaning of) refuge, (2) the going for refuge, (3) the one who goes for refuge, (4) the analysis of going for refuge, (5) the fruit of going for refuge, (6) the defilement, and (7) the breach.

(1) As to the *(meaning of) refuge* (*saraṇa*): it slays (*hiṃsati*), thus it is a refuge.[78] The meaning is that for those who have gone

---

78. The commentator here derives the word *saraṇa* unetymologically from a rare verb *sarati* meaning "to crush" or "to destroy" rather than from the common and etymologically correct *sarati* meaning "to run."

for refuge it kills and destroys their fear, terror, and suffering, and the affliction of (rebirth into) a bad destination. "Refuge" is a designation for the Triple Gem.

Or alternatively, the Buddha slays the fear of beings by promoting their welfare and by preventing their harm; the *Dhamma* does so by enabling them to cross the desert of existence and by giving them comfort, and the *Saṅgha* by making even small religious acts yield the gain of abundant fruit. Therefore, in this way too, the Triple Gem is a refuge.

(2) The *going for refuge* is an act of consciousness which, through confidence in and reverence for the Triple Gem, is devoid of defilements and occurs in the mode of regarding the Triple Gem as the supreme resort.

N. SUB. CY. "An act of consciousness" (*citt'uppāda*): the going for refuge is a consciousness conjoined with its associated phenomena such as faith and wisdom, etc., occurring in such a mode. It has confidence in the Triple Gem thus: "The Exalted One is perfectly enlightened, the *Dhamma* is well-expounded, the *Saṅgha* is practicing well." And it has reverence for the Triple Gem as well. Through that confidence and reverence it is "devoid of defilements," that is, it has shaken off such evil states as doubt, delusion, and lack of faith, etc. It regards "the Triple Gem as the supreme resort": the Triple Gem is its supreme resort, supreme goal, protection, and shelter.

Here, by mentioning *confidence*, the commentator indicates the mundane going for refuge, for that is dominated by faith, not by knowledge; by mentioning *reverence*, he indicates the supramundane going for refuge, for noble ones regard the Triple Gem with reverence through direct knowledge of its excellent qualities. Therefore, through such confidence the defilements are removed by way of abandonment by factor substitution, through such reverence they are removed by way of abandonment by eradicating the causes of irreverence. "Regarding the Triple Gem as the supreme resort" refers to all four kinds of going for refuge, to be explained below. Or else, without distinction, either term—confidence or reverence—can signify both the mundane and supramundane going for refuge. For the mention of confidence can imply both the unwavering confidence of the supramundane and the confidence still subject to wavering of the mundane. Similarly, the mention of reverence can imply both mundane and supramundane reverence.

CY. (3) The *one who goes for refuge* is a being endowed with that (act of consciousness). The meaning is one who approaches (the Triple Gem) with the aforesaid act of consciousness thus: "This Triple Gem is my refuge, this is my supreme resort."

(4) In the *analysis of the going for refuge*, the going for refuge is twofold, the supramundane and the mundane. The supramundane going for refuge is achieved at the moment of the path by those who have seen the truths,[79] through the eradication of the defilements of the going for refuge; by way of its object, it takes *Nibbāna* as its objects, and by way of its task, it succeeds in regard to the entire Triple Gem.

N. SUB. CY. "It takes *Nibbāna* as its object": when this is said, it is indicated that, in denotation, the achievement of the four truths or the knowledge of the path is itself the supramundane going for refuge. For therein, with the achievement of the four truths the defilements of the going for refuge are eradicated by way of the breakthrough of abandonment. The *Dhamma* as *Nibbāna* accomplishes the going for refuge when it is penetrated by way of the breakthrough of realization, and the *Dhamma* as the path does so when it is penetrated by way of the breakthrough of development. The excellent qualities of the Buddha which come into range (of the understanding) of disciples accomplish the going for refuge when they are penetrated by way of the breakthrough of full understanding; so too the excellent qualities of the noble *Saṅgha*. Thus he says, "it succeeds in regard to the entire Triple Gem."

CY. The mundane going for refuge is achieved by worldlings through the suppression of the defilements of the going for refuge; by way of its object, it takes as its object the excellent qualities of the Buddha, the *Dhamma*, and the *Saṅgha*. In denotation, it

79. This refers to the path of stream-entry, when the Four Noble Truths are directly seen and all doubt regarding the Triple Gem is eradicated.

is the gaining of faith in the objects of faith—the Buddha, etc.—and right view rooted in faith, referred to as the "straightening of view" among the ten bases of meritorious activity.

SUB. CY. "Right view rooted in faith": right view preceded by the aforesaid faith, (which arises) by seeing methodically, with mundane understanding, that the Buddha is well enlightened, that the *Dhamma* is well taught, and that the *Saṅgha* is practicing well. By this phrase the commentator shows that the mundane going for refuge is wisdom having the aforesaid characteristic and with faith as its decisive support. By the phrase "the gaining of faith" he shows the going for refuge dissociated from knowledge, as in the case of children who are prompted by their parents, etc.; by the phrase "right view" he shows the going for refuge associated with knowledge.

CY. This mundane going for refuge occurs in four ways: by self-surrender, by taking the Triple Gem as one's supreme resort, by the acceptance of pupilship, and by homage by prostration.[80]

Therein, *self-surrender* is the relinquishing of oneself to the Triple Gem, expressed thus: "From today onward I surrender myself to the Buddha, to the *Dhamma*, and to the *Saṅgha*." *Taking the Triple Gem as one's supreme resort* is expressed thus: "From today onward the Buddha is my supreme resort, the *Dhamma* is my supreme resort, the *Saṅgha* is my supreme resort. Thus may you know me!" *The acceptance of pupilship* is expressed thus: "From today onward I am a pupil of the Buddha, a pupil of the *Dhamma*, a pupil of the *Saṅgha*. Thus may you know me!" *Homage by prostration* is the quality of deepest humility towards the Buddha, the *Dhamma*, and the *Saṅgha*, expressed thus: "From today onward I do homage, rise up in respect, show reverential salutation, and perform the proper duties only towards the three objects of refuge: the Buddha, the *Dhamma*, and the *Saṅgha*. Thus may you know me!" Refuge is taken by acting in any of these four ways.

---

80. *Attasanniyyātana, taparāyanatā, sissabhāvupagamana, pānipāta.* For a modern account, see Nyanaponika Thera, *The Threefold Refuge* (BPS Wheel No. 76), pp. 20-26.

Further, *self-surrender* may be understood through such expressions as the following: "I relinquish myself to the Buddha, the *Dhamma*, and the *Saṅgha*. I relinquish my life to them. My self has been relinquished to them, my life has been relinquished to them. Until the end of my life, I go for refuge to the Buddha. The Buddha is my refuge, my shelter, my protection."

The acceptance of pupilship may be understood through the example of Mahākassapa's going for refuge, thus: "I would see the Teacher, the Exalted One! I would see the Accomplished One, the Exalted One! I would see the Perfectly Enlightened One, the Exalted One!" (SN 16:11/S II 220).

Taking the Triple Gem as one's supreme resort may be understood through the example of the going for refuge of Ālavaka, etc., thus;

From village to village
And town to town I'll wander
Venerating the Enlightened One
And his well-taught *Dhamma*. (Sn 192)

Homage by prostration may be illustrated thus: "Then the brahmin Brahmāyu rose up from his seat, arranged his upper robe over one shoulder, bowed down with his head at the Exalted One's feet, and kissed the Exalted One's feet with his mouth, stroked them with his hands, and declared his name, 'I am the brahmin Brahmāyu, honorable Gotama! I am the brahmin Brahmāyu, honorable Gotama!" (MN 91/M II 144).

Homage by prostration may be of four kinds: that shown towards a relative, that motivated by fear, that shown towards a teacher, and that based on esteem for spiritual worthiness. Of these, homage by prostration based on esteem for spiritual worthiness constitutes the going for refuge, not the others. For one takes refuge only by way of the highest and breaks it only by way of the highest.

Therefore, if a member of the Sākya or Koliya clan venerates the Buddha thinking, "He is our relative," he has not thereby taken refuge. Or if one venerates the Buddha out of fear, thinking, "The recluse Gotama is worshipped by kings and has great power; if I do not venerate him, he may harm me," one has not taken refuge. Or, upon remembering something one learned from the Exalted One during the time he was a *bodhisatta* or some mundane instruction one received from him after he became a Buddha, if one venerates him thinking, "He is my teacher," one has not taken refuge. But if one venerates the Buddha thinking, "He is the most worthy being in the world," one has taken refuge.

Conversely, if a man or woman lay follower who has taken refuge venerates a renunciant belonging to another sect, thinking, "He is my relative," his going for refuge is not broken; much less then is it broken in venerating one who is not a renunciant. So, too, the refuge is not broken if one venerates a king out of fear, thinking, "He is worshipped by all the country; if I do not venerate him, he may harm me." Nor if one venerates a sectarian teacher from whom one has learned a craft, thinking, "He is my teacher."

Thus the analysis of the going for refuge should be understood.

(5) *The fruit of going for refuge* should be understood as follows. In the case of the supramundane going for refuge [that is, the noble path], the four fruits of recluseship are the resultant-fruit,[81] the destruction of all suffering is the benefit-fruit. For this is said:

One who has gone for refuge to
The Buddha, *Dhamma*, and *Saṅgha*
Sees with perfect wisdom
The Four Noble Truths—

Suffering, the rise of suffering,
The transcending of suffering,
And the Noble Eightfold Path
That leads to the end of suffering—

This is the secure refuge,
This is the supreme refuge,

81. The fruits of stream-entry, the once-returner, the non-returner, and *arahatship*.

By relying on this refuge
One is released from all suffering. (Dhp 190–192)

Further, the benefit-fruit of the (supramundane) going for refuge may be understood by way of "not approaching any formations as permanent," etc. For this is said: "It is impossible, it cannot come to pass, that an individual who has attained to right view might approach any formation as permanent, any formation as pleasurable, any phenomenon as self. It is impossible, it cannot come to pass, that he might deprive his mother of life, that he might deprive his father of life, that he might deprive an *arahat* of life, that with a mind of hatred he might shed a *Tathāgata*'s blood, that he might create a schism in the *Saṅgha*, that he might point to someone other (than the Buddha) as his teacher. This is impossible" (MN 115/M III 65).

The fruit of the mundane going for refuge is the attainment of a (favorable) existence and the attainment of wealth. For this is said:

Those who have gone for refuge to the Buddha
Do not go to the plane of misery.
Having abandoned the human body,
They fill up the order of the gods. (SN 4:37/S I 27)

It is also said: "Then Sakka, the king of the gods, together with eighty-thousand deities approached venerable Mahāmoggallāna … who told him: 'It is good, O lord of the gods, to go for refuge to the Buddha. Because of going for refuge to the Buddha, some beings here, with the breakup of the body, reappear after death in a good destination, in a heavenly world. They surpass the other gods in ten respects: in divine life span, in divine beauty, in divine pleasure, in divine fame, in divine sovereignty, and in divine forms, sounds, smells, tastes, and tangibles'" (SN 40:10/S IV 275). The same method applies in going for refuge to the *Dhamma* and the *Saṅgha*. Further, the distinctive fruit of going for refuge should be understood by way of the Velāma Sutta, etc. [where the Buddha says that going for refuge is more fruitful than the most lavish acts of generosity (AN 9:20/A IV 395)].

CY. (6) In regard to *defilement*, the mundane going for refuge is defiled by ignorance, doubt, misunderstanding, etc., concerning the three objects of faith; thus it does not become very luminous and pervasive. But there is no defilement of the supramundane going for refuge.

(7) The *breach* of the mundane going for refuge is of two kinds, blameworthy and blameless. The blameworthy comes about when one surrenders oneself, etc., to another teacher, etc.; this has undesirable fruits. The blameless occurs when one dies; because this does not produce kammic results it is without fruit. But there is no breach of the supramundane going for refuge.

Thus the defilement and the breach of the going for refuge should be understood.

Let the Exalted One accept me as a lay follower

CY. The meaning is: "Let the Exalted One accept me thus, 'He is a lay follower'; let him know me thus."

Here, in order to gain proficiency with regard to the subject of the lay follower (*upāsaka*), the following miscellany should be understood: (1) Who is a lay follower? (2) Why is he called "lay follower"? (3) What is his moral discipline? (4) What is his livelihood? (5) What is his failure? (6) What is his success?

(1) Therein, who is a lay follower? Any householder who has gone for refuge. Thus it is said: "Mahānāma, when one has gone for refuge to the Buddha, the *Dhamma*, and the *Saṅgha*, to this extent one is a lay follower" (SN 55:37/S V 395).

(2) Why is he called "lay follower"? Because he has drawn near (*upāsanato*) to the Triple Gem. For he draws near (*upāsati*) to the Buddha, the *Dhamma*, and the *Saṅgha*—thus he is a lay follower (*upāsaka*).

(3) What is his moral discipline? The five abstinences. As it is said: "Mahānāma, when a lay follower abstains from the destruction of life, from taking what is not given, from sexual misconduct, from false speech, and from fermented and distilled intoxicants which are the basis for heedlessness, to this extent a lay follower is morally disciplined" (SN 55:37/S V 395).

(4) What is his livelihood? Having abandoned five kinds of wrong trade, he earns his living righteously, in accordance with the *Dhamma*. For this is said: "*Bhikkhus*, these five trades should not be engaged in by a lay follower. What five? Trading in weapons, trading in beings, trading in meat, trading in intoxicants, and trading in poisons. These are the five trades which should not be engaged in by a lay follower" (AN 5:177/A III 208).

(5) What is his failure? Failure in his moral discipline and in his livelihood, this is his failure, Further, that which makes him an outcast, stained and repulsive, that too is his failure. This refers to the five qualities, such as lack of faith, etc. As it is said "*Bhikkhus*, possessed of five qualities, a lay follower is an outcast lay follower, a stained lay follower, a repulsive lay follower. What five? He lacks faith; he is immoral; he believes in superstitious omens; he relies on omens, not on *kamma*; he seeks spiritually worthy persons outside of here [that is, outside the Buddha's dispensation] and he shows honor there first" (AN 5:175/A III 206).

(6) What is his success? Success in his moral discipline and success in his livelihood, this is his success. So too are the five qualities, such as faith, etc., which make him a gem, etc. As it is said: "*Bhikkhus*, possessed of five qualities, a lay follower is a gemlike lay follower, a red lotus-like lay follower, a white lotus-like lay follower. What five? He has faith; he is morally disciplined; he does not believe in superstitious omens; he relies on *kamma*, not on omens; he does not seek spiritually worthy persons outside of here and he shows honor here first" (AN 5:175/A III 206).

GONE FOR REFUGE FROM THIS DAY ONWARDS AS LONG AS I LIVE

CY. "As long as my life continues, for so long let the Exalted One accept me and know me as a steward, as a lay follower who has gone for refuge through the threefold going for refuge and does not recognize anyone else as the Teacher. If someone were to cut off my head with a sharp sword, even then I would not deny the Buddha, the *Dhamma*, or the *Saṅgha*."

VENERABLE SIR, A TRANSGRESSION OVERCAME ME

CY. Having thus gone for refuge by self-surrender, the king spoke this, revealing the crime he had committed.

102. FOR THIS, GREAT KING, IS GROWTH IN THE DISCIPLINE OF THE NOBLE ONE

CY. "This, great king, is called growth in the discipline of the Noble One, in the dispensation of the Exalted Buddha." What? Seeing one's transgression as a transgression, making amends for it according to the *Dhamma*, and achieving restraint in the future.

103. HE PAID HOMAGE TO THE EXALTED ONE, CIRCUMAMBULATED HIM THREE TIMES, AND DEPARTED

CY. Having circumambulated the Exalted One three times, he joined his hands in reverential salutation and placed them on his head, and retreated facing the Exalted One as long as he was in his range of sight. When he faded from sight, the king paid homage with all his limbs on the ground and departed.

104. THIS KING, *BHIKKHUS*, HAS RUINED HIMSELF

CY. This is meant: "This king, *bhikkhus*, has ruined himself, injured himself, and has destroyed his support. He has ruined himself by himself alone, in such a way that he has no support."

N. SUB. CY. The king has "ruined himself" by ruining the wholesome roots he achieved for himself in the past, which might have brought their results in this present existence itself. He has "injured himself" by injuring those wholesome roots. By these two terms, which are synonymous, the Buddha shows his criminal action. To show the ruin and injury through the destruction of his support—that is, of his wholesome roots—it is said "(he) has destroyed his support." "Support" (*patiṭṭhā*) is one in meaning with root; it is called support because it supports the descent into fixity of rightness (i.e. the supramundane path). Through his criminal action he has broken and destroyed his achievement of wholesome supporting conditions, thus he has "destroyed his support." Since his own support, his wholesome root, does not remain, the king has "ruined himself by himself alone."

IN THIS VERY SEAT THERE WOULD HAVE ARISEN IN HIM THE DUST-FREE, STAINLESS EYE OF *DHAMMA*

CY. It is "dust-free" because it is devoid of the dust of lust, etc., and "stainless" because of the absence of the stain of lust, etc. It is the "eye of *Dhamma*" in the sense that it is the eye seeing into phenomena (*dhammesu cakkhuṃ*), or the eye made by *Dhamma* (*dhammamayaṃ cakkhuṃ*). In other places this is a designation for the three [lower] paths, but here only for the path of stream-entry.

N. SUB. CY. "The eye seeing into phenomena": the eye is the path of stream-entry, so called because it has the meaning of "seeing"; "phenomena" are the phenomena of the Four Noble Truths, or the phenomena of the three lower paths.

"The eye made by *Dhamma*": the eye produced by *Dhamma*, that is, by the *Dhamma* of serenity and insight. Further, as the word "made" (*maya*) is used with the meaning of "consisting of," the Pali phrase can mean "the eye made of *Dhamma*," that is, consisting of the three aggregates of *Dhamma*—moral discipline, concentration, and wisdom.

CY. This is meant (by the above passage of the *sutta*): "If he had not murdered his father, while sitting here now in this very seat he would have attained the path of stream-entry. But because of associating with evil friends [Devadatta and his followers], an obstacle has arisen for him. Though such is the case, he has approached the *Tathāgata* and gone for refuge to the Triple Gem. Therefore, just as someone who has killed a man might be freed by paying a fine, so through the greatness of my dispensation, this king, having been born in the Hell of Copper Cauldrons, after falling downwards for thirty thousand years until he reaches the bottom and rising upwards for thirty thousand years until he again reaches the top, will be freed." This, it is said, was spoken by the Exalted One, though it has not been included in the text.

N. SUB. CY. "The Hell of Copper Cauldrons": for the beings who are to experience this realm, a large cauldron made of copper is produced by the power of their *kamma*. To go downwards to the bottom and upwards to the top takes altogether sixty thousand years. Other beings (reborn there) fall downwards and rise upwards again and again, and are tortured there for many hundred thousands of years. But not so this king. He will fall downwards and rise upwards only one time, in the way described, and having been tortured for only sixty thousand years, he will be freed.

CY. Having heard this *sutta*, did the king gain any benefit? He gained great benefit. For from the time he killed his father he did not get any sleep, either by night or by day. But from the time he approached the Teacher and heard this sweet nutritious teaching of the *Dhamma*, he was able to sleep. He showed great honor to the Triple Gem. There was no one equal to this king in possessing the faith of a worldling. And in the future he will become a *paccekabuddha* named Vijita and attain final *Nibbāna*.

SUB. CY. *Query*: If the king was not obstructed by his *kamma*, the eye of *Dhamma* would have arisen in him in that very seat. How, then, in the future could he become a *paccekabuddha* and attain final *Nibbāna*? On the other hand, if he will become a *paccekabuddha* and attain final *Nibbāna*, how was it that the eye of *Dhamma* could have arisen in him? Are not the decisive supports for the enlightenment of a disciple and the enlightenment of a *paccekabuddha* different supports?

Reply: There is no contradiction, for he will accumulate the requisites for the enlightenment of a *paccekabuddha* subsequent to this occasion. For those beings who might have awakened through the enlightenment of a disciple, if there was no opportunity to do so at an intermediary time, may awaken through the enlightenment of a *paccekabuddha* in the case when they make such an aspiration.

But others say that this king had already made the aspiration for the enlightenment of a *paccekabuddha*. For even though beings have made such an aspiration, if they have not become fixed in destiny (*niyati*), because their knowledge has not arrived at maturity they may attain the enlightenment of a disciple in the personal presence of the Teacher. Thus the Exalted One says, "*Bhikkhus*, if this king had not taken the life of his father," etc.

Only the great *bodhisattas* (those bound for Buddhahood) are freed from committing heinous crimes (such as parricide or matricide), not the other *bodhisattas*. Thus Devadatta, though fixed in destiny for the enlightenment of a *paccekabuddha*, generated even heavier evil *kamma* through his resentment toward the Buddha, the Protector of the World. Therefore, because of the obstacle of *kamma*, this king did not encounter the opportunity for the breakthrough of vision (into the truths), but being fixed in destiny for the enlightenment of a *paccekabuddha*, in the future he will become a *paccekabuddha* and attain final *Nibbāna*.

CY. Thus spoke the Exalted One. Elated in mind, the *bhikkhus* rejoiced in the Exalted One's words.

Concluded

ABOUT PARIYATTI

Pariyatti is dedicated to providing affordable access to authentic teachings of the Buddha about the *Dhamma* theory (*pariyatti*) and practice (*paṭipatti*) of Vipassana meditation. A 501(c)(3) nonprofit charitable organization since 2002, Pariyatti is sustained by contributions from individuals who appreciate and want to share the incalculable value of the *Dhamma* teachings. We invite you to visit www.pariyatti.org to learn about our programs, services, and ways to support publishing and other undertakings.

Pariyatti Publishing Imprints

Vipassana Research Publications (focus on Vipassana as taught by S.N. Goenka in the tradition of Sayagyi U Ba Khin)

BPS Pariyatti Editions (selected titles from the Buddhist Publication Society, copublished by Pariyatti)

MPA Pariyatti Editions (selected titles from the Myanmar Pitaka Association, copublished by Pariyatti)

Pariyatti Digital Editions (audio and video titles, including discourses)

Pariyatti Press (classic titles returned to print and inspirational writing by contemporary authors)

Pariyatti enriches the world by

- disseminating the words of the Buddha,
- providing sustenance for the seeker's journey,
- illuminating the meditator's path.

www.ingramcontent.com/pod-product-compliance
Lightning Source LLC
Chambersburg PA
CBHW031640040426
42453CB00006B/166
* 9 7 8 1 6 8 1 7 2 4 9 7 3 *